CATHOLICISM AND ADHD

Finding Holiness Depsite Distractions

Catholicism and ADHD: Finding Holiness Despite Destractions
Copyright © 2019 Reset ADHD, LLC

Published by Reset ADHD, LLC

ISBN: 978-0-578-54462-5

Dedicated to my fellow ADHDers
You are all awesome, and I love you

TABLE OF CONTENTS

PROLOGUE

In college, I had the time in my schedule most semesters to visit a local Adoration chapel every day. During those visits, I frequently found myself unable to focus. In those moments, I would get dejected, give up on praying, and leave the chapel. One day, I did not just get dejected. I was embarrassed, humiliated, and frustrated. My faith was (and still is) the most important aspect of my life, and I could not focus while praying. As tears filled my eyes, guilt and shame began to well up inside of me. One thought dominated my mind and refused to cease pestering me: What is wrong with me?

INTRODUCTION FOR ADHDᴇʀs

First of All...

If you are reading this because you suspect you have ADHD, skip to the chapter titled, "Get a Diagnosis!" This will be the most beneficial place for you to start. Getting an actual diagnosis for ADHD is important, and not doing so can be detrimental. I explain why in that chapter. Seriously, stop reading this, and either read "Get a Diagnosis!" or actually go out and get a diagnosis. You will thank me later.

If you have not been diagnosed with ADHD, stop reading this. You have your own introduction. Read that. Do not worry. We will not be saying rude things about you or sharing super-confidential ADHD secrets.

If you have been diagnosed with ADHD, read on!

The Actual Introduction to This Book for Those with ADHD

Doctor Peter Kreeft, one of my favorite authors, only writes books when he wants to read a book that has not been written. There needs to be a book for Catholics with ADHD. Right now, no one is addressing how to be a Catholic when you have ADHD. Those of us who are Catholics with ADHD face some unique challenges when it comes to our daily lives and practicing the Faith. I hope this book will help you in your efforts to manage ADHD and grow in holiness. If none of that works, I hope, at the very least, you can find some comfort in the fact that you are not alone.

Knowledge Is Key to ADHD Success

The simple fact you have picked up this book means you have taken an important step towards growth. Knowing more about the wild beast that is ADHD will give you the power to tame it. As the old saying goes, the first step in overcoming a problem is admitting there is a problem. I know I have grown while writing this book, and I hope some things I have learned will help you.

A Caveat

It should be noted that I am not a doctor nor a professional researcher and that a lot of what I have to say is based on my own experience as both an ADHDer and an ADHD coach and stuff I found on the internet. Everyone experiences ADHD in their own unique way. Your experiences may differ greatly from mine. What I want to accomplish through this book, though, is to let those of you with ADHD know that you are not alone, offer some tips on how a Catholic can better manage the symptoms of ADHD to improve their spiritual life, and inform those who do not have ADHD of the struggles we face and what they can do to assist us in our spiritual life.

How This Book Works

I have tried to write this book in an ADHD-friendly way. Like you probably do, I often go off on tangents while telling a story or otherwise conversing with others. As a result, this book will have a lot of footnotes.[1] Some footnotes will be informative, and others might be there simply to make you laugh.

I know what reading a book is like when your brain has ADHD. Therefore, I have tried to be as brief as possible, while still adequately explaining things, and I have broken down the chapters into sections. Also, I did not write this book in the order in which it appears in this book. I bounced around. I wrote a chapter here. Then, I would write a little bit of a couple of other chapters there. In short, you should feel free to bounce around this book and read those chapters you feel you most need to read at this point in time. As someone with ADHD, I know there is a good chance you will start this book and never finish. Make the most of the time you will spend with this book in your hand and read what will provide you with the most benefit.[2]

---

1 Hi! I do not have anything interesting or worthwhile to say here. I just wanted to introduce the concept.

2 The idea of writing a book in such a way that is friendly to the ADHD brain is an idea I stole from *Delivered from Distraction* by Doctors Edward M. Hallowell and John J. Ratey, a book I highly recommend.

INTRODUCTION FOR NON-ADHDERS

It Is Real

If you believe ADHD exists, you may skip this paragraph. If you do not believe ADHD is real, I have a few words for you. ADHD's existence has been scientifically proven. If you deny ADHD exists, you deny science, and you deny Church teaching, which clearly states truth cannot contradict truth. Bottom line: ADHD exists, and it makes no sense to refute it.

Now that we are all on the same page, let us begin.

There Is No Cure

Did you pick up this book hoping to find a cure for ADHD? Sorry, no cure for ADHD exists. Your loved one will always have ADHD. Some people incorrectly believe children grow out of ADHD, but this is not true. There are some lucky individuals who no longer experience the symptoms of ADHD in adulthood,[3] but this is a rarity.

I Offer No Alternative Treatments

Did you pick up this book hoping to find a way to treat ADHD without medication? Sorry, I cannot offer that. The only treatment method that has been scientifically proven to help reduce the symptoms of ADHD is medication. Yes, therapy, coaching, educational accommodations, and other interventions can help manage symptoms, but those symptoms will still exist and will continue to cause your loved one's difficulties. Furthermore, concerns that taking medication for ADHD increases the likelihood that a person will become addicted to drugs are unfounded. Research[i] has shown that those with ADHD who have taken medication are less likely to become addicted to drugs than those with ADHD who have not taken medication[4]. In short, if you refuse to try medication for a loved one, you are refusing to try the best treatment option. That said, however, medication does not work for some people, and for others, the side effects of medication outweigh the benefits they receive from the medication. Most healthcare

---

3   My unscientific opinion is that these individuals have a less severe case of ADHD and years of coping with it has trained them to manage the symptoms of ADHD better. Again, I am not a doctor or even a scientist. I put this opinion in the footnote and not the main text because of the minuscule amount of information I used in formulating this opinion.

4   Those with ADHD who are not medicated often get addicted to drugs or alcohol because they self-medicate.

professionals[5] recommend medication, along with non-medicinal interventions like therapy or coaching.

This Book Might Be For You If...

Did you pick up this book looking for an understanding of those (perhaps someone you love) with ADHD? Do you want to know you can do for someone with ADHD to help them succeed in life and grow in their spiritual life? If so, this book is for you. Read on!

A Word of Warning

This book was written in a manner intended to cater to those with ADHD. The chapters are brief.[6] There are footnotes aplenty, which mimics how an ADHD brain can often go on random tangents when explaining something or telling a story. Also, this book might seem unprofessional because of the zany sense of humor used throughout and the inclusion of personal pronouns.[7]

A Caveat

It should be noted that I am not a doctor nor a professional researcher and that a lot of what I have to say is based on my own experience both as an ADHDer and an ADHD coach, and research I have done on my own. Everyone experiences ADHD in their own unique way. Your loved one's experiences may differ greatly from mine. It is my hope, though, that this book will let those with ADHD know that they are not alone, offer some tips on how a Catholic can better manage the symptoms of ADHD to improve their spiritual life, and inform those who do not have ADHD of the struggles we face and what they can do to assist us in our spiritual life.

---

5   When I say, "Most healthcare professionals," what I really mean is, "Most healthcare professionals who actually know what the heck they are talking about when it comes to ADHD." Sadly, too few of these individuals actually exist.

6   Some chapters that were meant to be one chapter were split up to make them shorter.

7   I was told in school to avoid using personal pronouns in my writing. Apparently, it is unprofessional or informal.

PART ONE: THE CROSS

WHAT IS ADHD?

"I praise You, because I am wonderfully made; wonderful are Your works! My very self You know." – Psalm 139:14

ADHD Defined

In any discussion, it is of the utmost importance to define one's terms so that everyone is on the same page. To make sure we are all on the same page as we go through this book, we need to make sure we all have the same understanding of what ADHD is and what it is not.[8]

Attention Deficit Hyperactivity Disorder (ADHD) is a neurodevelopmental disorder[9] characterized by inattention, hyperactivity, and impulsivity.[10] It is important to note these three characteristics must be present for longer than six months and cause impairments and dysfunction in more than one area of a person's life (e.g. school, work, home, etc.). The DSM-V requires that these symptoms are or were present before the age of 12.[11]

ADHD manifests in one of three main presentations: predominately hyperactive-impulsive, predominately inattentive, and a combined presentation. The predominately hyperactive-impulsive type is the person who constantly fidgets, interrupts others, cannot sit still, and appears as if they are driven by a motor. The predominately inattentive type[12] (formerly known as ADD) is the person who spaces out in conversations, homilies, or lectures; fails to follow through on directions; is forgetful; loses things; and is unorganized. I like to say that the inattentive type is exactly like the hyperactive-impulsive type, except the hyperactivity is confined to the mind.[13] The combined type is a combination of the hyperactive-impulsive and inattentive types.

Executive Function Dysfunction

ADHD causes extreme problems with executive functions, and this executive function dysfunction is one of the main reasons for the struggles ADHDers face. Inattention and hyperactivity can be more easily regulated than

---

8   ADHDers, bear with me on this one. I wrote this chapter mainly for the non-ADHDers. Feel free to skip this chapter. I know you know what ADHD is, but if you would like a refresher or a deeper understanding, read on!

9   According to the DSM-V, neurodevelopmental disorders are characterized by impairments that affect a person's personal, social, academic, or occupational activities that usually manifest during early development.

10   The DSM-V combines hyperactivity and impulsivity into one characteristic. So, in the DSM-V, there are two main characteristics of ADHD, not three.

11   There is some leeway to this, especially when diagnosing an adult. Memories can be hard to accurately recall as an adult or even as a teen.

12   In case you were curious, this is the one I have.

13   This is why ADD and ADHD were combined into one disorder. The two types both experience hyperactivity, just in different ways.

executive function troubles. Executive functions affect our school, work, and home lives, and messing up in these areas causes serious problems.

The definition of and list of executive functions varies depending on who is defining and listing them. A good general description of executive functions is those tasks that help you get things done and control yourself. Common executive functions that are impaired by ADHD include impulse control, self-monitoring, emotional control, moving from one task to another, verbal and nonverbal working memory, time management, and organization.

Different Wiring

An important concept to explain when describing ADHD is that ADHD brains are wired differently. This is useful for helping those with ADHD and those without ADHD understand that the difficulties caused by ADHD are not caused by stupidity, laziness, or a lack of effort. There are demonstrable differences between ADHD and non-ADHD brains, and as the technology that allows scientists to study the brain improve, we are able to see the differences between ADHD brains and neurotypical brains better.

Studies have shown that there are structural abnormalities in ADHD brains. A 2005 review[ii] noted that, in studies conducted on children with ADHD, researchers have consistently found that the dorsolateral prefrontal cortex, caudate, pallidum, corpus callosum, and cerebellum are smaller in ADHD brains. A 2007 meta-analysis[iii] found that the "[r]egions most frequently assessed and showing the largest differences included cerebellar regions, the splenium of the corpus callosum, total and right cerebral volume, and right caudate. Several frontal regions assessed in only two studies also showed large significant differences."

Aside from structural differences, there are also functional differences in ADHD brains. For example, a 2005 study[iv] found "significantly reduced brain activation in the right inferior prefrontal cortex during successful motor response inhibition and in the precuneus and posterior cingulate gyrus during inhibition failure, both of which correlated with behavioral scores of ADHD." In 2001, Doctor Marcus Raichle made what could be[14] one of the most profound neurological discoveries ever. He noticed that brains not engaged in a task had certain areas[15] increase their metabolic activity and called these areas the "default mode network." When the brain is engaged in a task, other areas of the brain increased their metabolic activity. Doctor Raichle called these other areas the "task-positive network." In neurotypical brains, these networks have a reciprocal relationship. The default mode network decreases when the task-positive network increases and vice versa. However, in ADHD brains, there is no reciprocity. The default mode network (which is responsible for things that do not require a conscious effort to focus like conjuring up a memory or daydreaming) remains active when the task-positive network increases its metabolic activity[v]. This lack of balance[16] between these two networks makes it difficult to focus on the task at hand.

---

14   I say "what could be" because there have been critics of this theory who have published reasons why they do not believe Doctor Raichle's theories. Although, a majority of scientists seem to support the idea of a "default mode network."

15   The medial prefrontal cortex, the posterior cingulate cortex, the hippocampus, the amygdala, and parts of the inferior parietal lobe

16   There is speculation that those adults who seem to have grown out of ADHD have developed a balance between the networks that

Floating Attention

One way to describe what ADHD feels like is "floating attention." The term "floating attention" is what some experts use to describe the way the brain works when it is trying to pay attention to as much as possible. These experts say that this could relate back to the days when humans were not at the top of the food chain and needed to be on guard against attacks from wild animals.

In my personal opinion, "floating attention" is an appropriate description of what ADHD is like. I know that, as I experience thoughts and try to focus on one thing, it can be hard for me to grasp the one thing on which I want to place my focus. My thoughts feel like they are floating around in my head, and I feel like I am desperately trying to keep all the ones in my head that I would like. If I am not careful, certain thoughts will float away, and even if that thought is not the thing on which I need to focus, I do not want to lose it. I want to be able to tie my thoughts down to anchor points in my brain and come back to them when I am ready to deal with them, but my brain is not equipped to do that. It is a constant battle to try to control my rambunctious thoughts.

Hyperfocus

Hyperfocus is a state of intense focus that those with ADHD experience. The ADHD brain can focus on a subject so much that everything else seems to disappear. It can be hard to break out of this state and move on to something else. Hyperfocus can mean rearranging the furniture right when the impulse to do so hits and not resting until the furniture is in a more pleasing arrangement. That may sound like a positive thing, but it is not pleasant when the urge to rearrange the furniture hits you just before midnight and keeps you up until 2:00 AM.[17] Hyperfocus can also take place with just our own emotions and thoughts. We can hold on to and focus on our emotional thoughts too much. This could lead to troubles with others if we cling to an argument too long. More tragically, it could lead to spending too much time criticizing one's own faults.[18]

Wait, Is It Floating Attention or Hyperfocus?

ADHD presents with a weird effect on one's ability to focus. Floating attention is one aspect of ADHD, and hyperfocus is another. They may seem like polar opposites, but they both accurately describe the ADHD experience. When one looks at both of these aspects of ADHD, a new perspective of ADHD emerges. It is not that those of us with ADHD cannot focus; it is that we cannot regulate where our focus is placed. A better name for attention deficit hyperactivity disorder might be attention regulation hyperactivity disorder.

---

neurotypicals have.

17   He wrote, speaking from personal experience.

18   I write more on negative self-talk in the chapter, "Shame."

Memory

Remember that thing you told a person with ADHD two seconds ago? Chances are, they do not. Those of us with ADHD have a poor working memory, which is the part of short-term memory that deals with immediate processing. That thing we were just holding and set down, like, two seconds ago that we could not possibly misplace somehow goes missing all the time. If you give us a set of instructions containing six parts and we do not write down all six parts, we will be lucky to remember one or two.[19] It can be difficult even to keep a thought in our brain long enough to be able to address it. That is why a person who has ADHD will frequently have a bunch of internet tabs and windows open at the same time.[20] We want to be able to remember that thing we wanted to look up on the internet after we finish looking at that thing on which we should currently be working which we will get back to after finishing watching that YouTube video we just remembered existed. These memory problems are among the most significant frustrations a person with ADHD faces on a daily basis.

Dopamine

Dopamine is the neurotransmitter that rewards the brain. The brain loves dopamine and wants more of it. The ADHD brain lacks the required levels of dopamine. Therefore, in the ADHD brain, there is a craving to get more dopamine.

Studies have shown those with ADHD do not have adequate dopamine receptors and transporters in the reward centers of the brain. As a result of the lack of dopamine, those with ADHD are less drawn to normal levels of rewards, and when they do receive those rewards, it is not as satisfying.[21] The shortage of rewards might cause ADHDers to subconsciously seek out activities that will be more rewarding and provide them with more dopamine.[22]

This might explain to some parents out there why their child with ADHD can focus on video games but not their school work or chores. ADHD brains crave dopamine. The reward centers of our brain respond better to the almost instant rewards[23] we get in video games.[24]

---

19   I remember being in elementary school and hearing directions from the teacher about our next activity, listening to every word, and then turning to the person next to me and saying, "What did she say?" I found this odd because I was paying attention and heard everything she said. This happened to me on more than one occasion.

20   This is also a popular metaphor for all of the thoughts that are in an ADHD brain at the same time. However, the tabs and windows make the ideas seem organized, and I can assure you they are not.

21   Some scientists refer to this as Reward Deficiency Syndrome (something non-ADHDers can have too).

22   Similar to how the ADHD brain needs dopamine, the ADHD person needs stimulation. Part of the reason people with ADHD are hyperactive may be explained by low arousal theory. This theory states that the base level of arousal for ADHDers is so low that the ADHD person must do something to stimulate arousal and compensate for the lack of arousal they receive from their surrounding environment. The result is hyperactive behavior.

23   Delayed gratification? Never heard of it! OK, I have, but those of us with ADHD struggle mightily to delay gratification.

24   NOTE: This is not a recommendation of video games for people with ADHD. I only mention video games because being rewarded quickly in video games is more appealing to ADHDers than studying for a test that is in two days that will help you get a good final grade at the end of the semester that will help get you into a college that will help you get a degree that will help you get a job that will help you pay for a family and a mortgage (or so they say). Rapid methods for acquiring dopamine are not always the healthiest methods. For example,

If you want to motivate your child with ADHD (or even your spouse with ADHD), try gamifying doing homework or completing chores. Gamifying school work and chores will provide a way to keep your child with ADHD stimulated and feel less compelled to seek out video games or other activities that provide instant dopamine. Provide the ADHDer with frequent rewards for completing the task you want them to do. Just make sure you explain to them you will only reward them when they do it right. Do not reward them for completing the task just to get it done. This will not help them develop a good work ethic. Also, it will be a source of tension for the two of you if they do not understand that you need the task to be done well. For everyone's sake, clearly define the requirements for receiving rewards.

The need for rewards also explains why ADHDers are prone to engaging in dangerous activities. We drive too fast, climb things we should not climb,[25] and do other things that make our mothers cringe. If you love someone with ADHD, help them find activities and hobbies that are highly rewarding but will not put their safety in jeopardy.[26]

Boredom

Those with ADHD need to be stimulated. The lack of dopamine in our systems means we frequently do battle with the boredom monster. There is a need to do something. The ADHD brain is repulsed by doing nothing. This results in an inner restlessness during inactivity leading to boredom, and the high occurrence of boredom in people with ADHD leads to some bizarre behavior. For example, when listening to music on the radio or on one's phone, most people who do not have ADHD listen to a song from beginning to end, but it is not uncommon for an ADHDer to move on to the next song before the song is even halfway done.[27] Boredom in those with ADHD can also lead to the ADHDer frequently changing jobs.[28] Those are just two examples of unusual behavior. If you check with someone with ADHD or someone who knows someone with ADHD, you will probably find more examples of bizarre, boredom-fighting behavior. If you know someone with ADHD, you might already know what I mean.

---

cocaine and heroin provide an instant and complete dopamine release, and I most certainly do not recommend street drugs to anyone. However, there is nothing wrong with playing video games every once in a while.

25   I spent one semester of college in Winona, Minnesota. If you have never been to Winona, it is a college town. There is nothing to do on the weekends except drink. While attending school there, I met a guy who, like me, did not drink, so his form of weekend entertainment was to climb buildings, not using stairs or ladders, but scaling the building using things like ledges or drainpipes to get on the roof. He took me out with him one night, and we got on top of most of the buildings on campus that night. When I transferred to a different school, I continued climbing buildings on my new campus (once dressed as Batman), something I did until a dislocated shoulder and an almost completely torn labrum (an injury that occurred, not while climbing buildings, but while deflecting a pass in a flag football game) forced me to retire from climbing buildings.

26   I believe it is important to explain here that an ADHD mind will always want to explore its latest extreme fascination or obsession. It is best to help your loved one find good and/or safe fascinations and obsessions.

27   There are many songs I can sing word-for-word during the first half to two-thirds of the song and have no clue what the lyrics are towards the end of the song.

28   The inability to complete tasks might also cause a person with ADHD to switch jobs often but not by choice.

Making and keeping friends is difficult when one has ADHD.[29] Our ADHD brains do not have the same wiring as neurotypical brains. Until we get a diagnosis, we may not know that a medical condition causes these differences, but we can tell others are different from us. We feel different,[30] and this causes us to be hesitant and unsure of ourselves in social situations. When trying to start a new friendship (and especially when trying to start a romantic relationship), there are few things one can do that are worse than overthinking[31] things and doubting oneself.

Complicating matters further is the way inattention can ruin our ability to pick up on social cues. The ADHDer does not notice the things that people do subtly to let others know how they are feeling. Our inability to place our focus completely on others causes us to miss nonverbal cues as to what others are thinking or how they are feeling.

Furthermore, other people can find it hard to accept ADHDers for who they are. The inability to control our focus can make others feel like we are not paying attention to them. It is not that we are not interested in what the other person has to say, but our struggle to place our focus on the potential friend and keep it there can give the impression that we do not care what they have to say. If a person does not understand this struggle with focus, we can find ourselves being rejected.[32] Another thing that causes people to reject a person with ADHD is the ADHDer's sense of humor. Those of us with ADHD tend to have zany senses of humor.[33] The things we find funny or the jokes we tell are off-the-wall, strange, and not funny to others. Yet, we cannot help but indulge this unusual side of ourselves. Lastly, our propensity to speak before thinking can cause some uncomfortable situations.

The struggle to fit in with peers can have consequences other than simply feeling left out, rejected, or lonely. When they do not have the natural propensity for making and keeping friends, a person with ADHD might try to do things to attract the attention and admiration of others. This could mean being the class clown, cracking jokes at inappropriate times during school, or exhibiting other rule-breaking behaviors. More dangerously, it could mean taking risks to impress others and engaging in daredevil-type activities.

Moreover, our fickleness causes those of us with ADHD to struggle to maintain already established friendships. When a new relationship begins, we can put a lot of effort into the relationship or even hyperfocus on it, but then, as time goes on, the newness wears off, causing it to be less exciting than it once was. The relationship may still be important, but the focus (and, in some cases, hyperfocus) has shifted to other relationships and/or activities, leaving the other party feeling neglected. In addition to the effort we put into relationships, our interests and hobbies

---

29   And, it is even harder when you are an introvert, like me.

30   I go more into this in the chapter entitled "Emotional Struggles."

31   Overthinking things could be considered hyperfocusing on our own insecurities.

32   And, that sucks. See "Emotional Struggles" for more information on that.

33   When I read in Doctors Edward Hallowell and John Ratey's *Delivered from Distraction* that a zany sense of humor was something characteristic of a person with ADHD, I thought to myself, *That explains so much*. Something that has, at times, alienated me from others finally made sense.

can also affect our relationships. As discussed below, a person with ADHD changes their hobbies often. When we move from hobby to hobby, friends with whom we enjoyed one hobby might get left behind when we move on to something new.

Rapidly Changing Hobbies and Interests

One day, while at a restaurant, I saw a man making balloon animals, and I thought to myself, *I can do that.* I did some research and ordered some balloon twisting equipment online. After popping many, many balloons, I mastered the craft[34] and became quite talented at taking balloons and making them appear like anything I wanted to make[35]. I would spend hours making balloon animals in high school on Friday and Saturday nights,[36] but once I got into college, I stopped balloon twisting almost entirely. I still enjoy making balloon animals and can do some cool things with 260s,[37] but I do not take the time to sit down and make some creative designs like I used to do. My interest in dedicating a lot of time to that hobby has waned. Exploring the balloon twisting world led me to explore other aspects of what I refer to as "the circus arts." I soon found myself gaining an interest in juggling, ventriloquism, and unicycles. I was able to teach myself how to juggle three balls, and I intended to learn how to juggle four balls, then five balls, and clubs as well. However, I never got the hang of juggling four balls, which made juggling five balls highly unlikely, if not impossible. I also moved into an apartment where the ceiling was too low to juggle clubs.[38] Learning ventriloquism was a complete bust, and my mom would not let me buy a unicycle.[39]

My movement from one hobby to the next is a perfect example of how a person with ADHD can have grand intentions of picking up a new hobby but failing to stick with it. We soon become bored and move on to the next hobby. This also affects projects we intend to do. Whether it is picking up yet another hobby, trying some activity we have always wanted to try, writing the next great American novel,[40] or starting a business, those with ADHD just cannot find it in themselves to finish what we start. We start many different projects[41] but finish few of them.[42]

---

34 You should see my dragon. IT. IS. EPIC.

35 There is a saying in the balloon twisting world that, once you learn to make a balloon dog, you can make anything. That is not exactly true, but the sentiment is accurate. Once you master the basic twists, what you can make is limited only by your imagination.

36 No, I was not getting paid to make balloons at a party. I just enjoyed making balloon sculptures and did not have much of a social life.

37 260s are the standard balloon twisting balloons. The 2 means there is a two-inch diameter of a fully inflated balloon, and the 60 means the length of a fully inflated balloon is 60 inches.

38 I have since moved into a house with tall enough ceilings for that, but I have not made a serious effort in learning to juggle clubs.

39 Not allowing me to get a unicycle was one of the best decisions my mom ever made. She knew I would have ended up getting hurt. Balance was never my strong suit, as is evidenced by my failed experiment with riding a moped that lasted less than a day (a story too long for a footnote).

40 Something I have always wanted to do but have never actually come close to doing

41 We are creative. New ideas come easy to us. Granted, not all of them are good ideas, but we have no shortage of ideas.

42 If you are reading this, I did a thing! I actually finished a project. Huzzah! +10 points to me!

Motivation and Procrastination

Possibly because of boredom but also possibly just due to the fickleness and/or the difficulties ADHD can cause, those with ADHD often experience a lack of motivation. We struggle to find sufficient motivation to do the task we need to do or the things we need to do at work, in school, or in our relationships. It is not that we do not want to do those things; it is that we cannot find the motivation to actually do it.[43] The effort we would need to put into the task seems greater than the consequences of not doing it. Desire in a person with ADHD does not always equate to the necessary motivation to do something. The lack of motivation leads to procrastination, which leads to a mad scramble to finish a project just before a deadline,[44] which leads to sloppy and subpar work.

Time Blindness

I know I cannot be the only person with ADHD who has ever had this happen to them:

Looks at watch

"I have plenty of time before I need to leave for that thing."

Looks at watch what seems like two seconds later

"SHOOT! [45] I need to leave NOW!"

Sprints to get in the car

Incidents like this are symptomatic of what has been given the nickname "time blindness." Simply put, those of us with ADHD have no concept of time. We regularly underestimate how long doing that one last thing before leaving the house will take. This makes it difficult to be punctual.

Organization

Organization does not exist in people with ADHD for the most part. It is not in our nature to be organized. Because of our inability to focus, remember things, and to sense how much time has passed, organization is contrary to the way our brains work. It takes a great deal of effort for us to get organized. ADHDers who are organized have spent a large amount of time developing strategies and systems for organization. For example, a person with ADHD might make a bunch of lists to help them remember things.[46] The way these people stay organized might seem strange to those without ADHD. But, other people with ADHD will see the wisdom in how they organize themselves and will be jealous of their system. However, if they try to emulate that person's system, there is a good chance it will not work to get them organized because no two people experience ADHD in the same way, and therefore, no two

---

43   This is faulty logic, but nevertheless, it persists in causing us to procrastinate.

44   Or sometimes after the deadline.

45   Confession time: I do not always say, "Shoot."

46   My family used to make fun of me for all of the lists I created. I now know that I wrote all of those lists because I was trying to cope with undiagnosed ADHD and the lists helped me remember things.

people with ADHD have the same organizational needs.

Not Everyone Experiences ADHD in the Same Way

Each unique person with ADHD deals with ADHD in a unique way. No one person experiences the symptoms of ADHD in the same way. ADHD also exists on a spectrum. Some have more extreme impairments than others. These differences in experiences for those with ADHD makes it difficult to describe ADHD to others adequately.[17][48]

---

47   So, if I am failing miserably at describing ADHD, this is a major reason why.

48   Moreover, the differences in the effect of ADHD make it difficult to treat ADHD adequately. When medicating a patient with ADHD, a doctor is forced to experiment with medication and dosages because of how unpredictable responses to ADHD medication can be

WHAT ADHD IS NOT

"Before I formed you in the womb I knew you." – Jeremiah 1:5

It's Myth Busting Time!

There are a lot of misconceptions about ADHD out there, and it is important to clear them up. If ADHD was understood properly, there would be more understanding of the challenges facing Catholics with ADHD, and ministries offered by the Church would be able to serve Catholic ADHDers better. It is imperative that myths about ADHD are busted, so the Church can better serve her people.

It Is Not Casual

In recent years, tremendous strides have been made in the mental health field. However, these efforts are being thwarted by those who do not take conditions like ADHD seriously. ADHD is not occasional, minor inattention. If you are prone to saying, "If I don't get my coffee, it's like I have ADHD or something," or "We all get a little ADHD sometimes," stop it. Just stop it. S-T-O-P new word I-T![49] When people casually refer to themselves as having ADHD, they minimize the struggles of those who do suffer from disorders like ADHD.

I do not wish to vilify those who casually use the term ADHD. I am not a member of the "Politically Correct Police." My point is to illustrate that there is a lot of ignorance with regards to mental health issues and that comments like these hurt the efforts of those trying to bring awareness to these issues.

There is little scientists know about ADHD, and when ADHD is treated as a joke, it becomes difficult to organize serious efforts to study and learn more about this disorder. When I tell people that I have ADHD, I worry that they might not actually realize I am being serious.[50] People whose lives are disrupted by ADHD already suffer enough. They do not need an additional struggle added on top of their current issues. To make their lives easier, we should all strive to only use the term ADHD to describe ADHD.[51]

It Is Not Caused by Food, Parents, or Technology

ADHD is caused by genetics.[52] This means no amount of sugar can cause hyperactivity,[vi] and there is no

---

49   +10 points if you caught the reference

50   A friend once said to me, "Wait, you actually have ADHD? I thought that was just a joke."

51   The same goes for terms like OCD or dyslexia.

52   There is no one ADHD gene. Heritability is a complicated issue. ADHD is the result of a combination of different genetic factors and reactions.

way to remove ADHD symptoms by changing a person's diet.[53] Also, ADHD is not caused by bad parenting.[54] Let me repeat that: ADHD is not caused by bad parenting.[55] Lastly, ADHD is not caused by too much screen time. Yes, too much time in front of a screen is a bad thing, but it does not cause ADHD. In fact, one can utilize one's technological devices to help manage ADHD. The technological advancements of phones now enable us to set reminders on our phones to help remember to do certain things, create checklists, and the list continues to grow as app developers continue to be more and more creative.[56]

It Is Not Fake

I know addressed this in the "Introduction for Non-ADHDers," but people often skip the introductions to books. Therefore, I feel compelled to address this topic again.

There are still people who do not believe ADHD is a real medical condition. The people who believe this deny science. Science has proven gravity exists, and no one doubts that. Science has proven that we need oxygen to breathe, and no one doubts that. Science has proven that ADHD exists, yet a large number of people believe that it does not exist. What gives?

I am not going to spend any time proving that ADHD exists. Science has proven it. ADHD has been documented for a lot longer than people realize. I have no intention of writing a proof for the existence of ADHD. Either you believe ADHD, or you deny science.

It Is Not an Excuse

I do not want to be given allowances or free passes because I have ADHD. What I want more than anything is to be normal. If I sin because of something related to having ADHD, I do not want to be automatically forgiven without seeking forgiveness and vowing not to sin again. I want to control my ADHD symptoms better in order to prevent me from sinning in the first place. Give me the accommodations I need to have a level playing field, but do not coddle me. The goal in any ADHD treatment plan is to get the person with ADHD to live as normal a life as possible. Yes, those of us with ADHD will mess up more than others, and you should be compassionate with us when we do so. But, do not allow us to accept anything less than the best. The long (and incomplete) list of successful people in the chapter entitled "Reasons for Hope" prove that ADHD is not a condemnation to a life of mediocrity. It serves as an example of the fact that we can be successful; it is a beacon of hope.

---

53 Eating a healthy diet is always a good choice and will benefit a person in many different ways, but a poor diet is not responsible for ADHD.

54 If your child has ADHD, there is no reason to feel guilty. Nothing you did caused him/her to have ADHD.

55 So, if you are judgmental of parents of children with ADHD, stop it. Just stop it.

56 But, yeah, the apps on a phone can be a source of hyperfocus. For example, as of the writing of these words, the Settlers of Catan app on my phone has accounted for 12% of my phone's battery usage over the past seven days, and I have gotten better about not playing it all the time.

It Is Not a Children's Issue

Adults suffer from ADHD, too. Many people believe ADHD is something kids have and will grow out of it by the time they reach adulthood. In reality, ADHD rarely goes away before adulthood. Many adults unknowingly have ADHD, and the consequences of undiagnosed ADHD are more dramatic for adults. Adult ADHD is tragically under diagnosed. One estimate[vii] states that 75% of adults with ADHD do not have a diagnosis.

It Is Not a Boy's Condition

Both genders can have ADHD. However, ADHD is more likely to go undiagnosed in females.[57] The exact reasons behind this are not clear. One of the leading theories is that girls are more likely to have the predominately inattentive type which goes undiagnosed more often than the hyperactive-impulsive type. Another prominent theory is that boys are more rambunctious in general which gets them in trouble more which leads to a closer examination of their behavior.

It Cannot Be Fixed

One of the things I was often told growing up was that I needed to try harder in school. I never understood what that meant. I was trying, yet my teachers and especially my mom[58] thought I should have been receiving better grades. I could not try harder; I was already giving my best effort.

Telling someone with ADHD to try harder does not help. ADHD cannot be fixed. It cannot be turned off. We will suffer from this condition as long as God wills us to do so. For most people, it is a life-long struggle.

---

57   ADHD is already under-diagnosed. This means girls with ADHD face a significantly more difficult battle in coping with ADHD.

58   My mom and I have both come a long way in our understanding of ADHD. She is a teacher and tries hard to accommodate her students with ADHD, which warms this ADHDer's heart. We butted heads back then because she saw my potential. She wanted me to succeed.

P.S. I love you, Mom.

GET A DIAGNOSIS!

"[Y]ou will know the truth, and the truth will set you free." – John 8:32

My Story and the Lessons Therein

As described in the prologue to this book, I visited a local Adoration chapel almost every day in the months leading up to the first time I sought an ADHD diagnosis. When I could not understand my inability to focus on the most important aspect of my life, I thought, What is wrong with me? I felt there was something amiss within me, but in reality, it was just a different brain wiring.

My story illustrates the importance of getting an ADHD diagnosis. Before getting diagnosed, I would get down on myself for not paying attention during prayer. Every stupid rabbit hole my brain went down while I was spaced out felt like a damning piece of evidence against my Christianity. If I truly loved God above all else, should not my focus have been on Him and Him alone? It is quite apparent now that I too easily gave into thoughts that were not inspired by the Holy Spirit or my guardian angel. Instead, I listened to the voice of the evil one telling me that I was not good enough or that I was failing the Lord. If I had continued to listen to that voice, I probably would no longer be practicing my faith. Instead, I recognized that something needed to change and sought an explanation for my lack of focus.

Through my ADHD diagnosis, I came to understand that God does not condemn me for my lack of focus in prayer. I am the person He made me to be. He made me with ADHD. Therefore, I am not ashamed to have ADHD.

Do not misunderstand me. ADHD is not an excuse. Yes, there is something I cannot control plaguing my prayer life, but I will not let myself think it is okay to just accept the fact that I cannot focus in prayer. I need to focus in prayer, so I will continue to control my ADHD as much as I can so that I might grow as close to the Lord as I can. The Lord understands when I cannot focus in prayer, but if I do not even try to focus or give up focusing on prayer entirely, then He begins to be concerned.

Moreover, the problems caused by ADHD need to be addressed for one to live a fulfilling life. A 2017 study[viii] noted that "ADHD symptoms were associated with significantly lower quality of life, lower self-esteem, higher emotional dysregulation, higher impulsivity questionnaire scores, more problematic internet use, greater occurrence of psychiatric disorders, and impaired stop-signal reaction times." All of these issues can cause major disruptions in a person's life, but they cannot be addressed until one seeks a diagnosis and begins a treatment plan.

Unmerited Shame and Frustration

As the story of my diagnosis process demonstrates, having undiagnosed ADHD can wreak havoc on one's emotional state and one's perception of oneself. If you feel like there is good reason to think you might have ADHD, go find out for sure. No good can come from not knowing or being unsure. Trust me, the lack of diagnosis will only hurt you in the long run. When you do not have a diagnosis, all of the blame for failures will land squarely on your shoulders. There will be no condition to mitigate the struggles you face every day. You will blame yourself for things that you cannot control, and that is not healthy.

Compounding Struggles

The struggles an ADHDer faces cannot be properly addressed if a diagnosis does not happen. Focusing will still be a major issue. Impulsivity will continue to cause embarrassing and/or dangerous situations. Hyperactivity will still cause difficulties sitting still. Time management will continue to seem impossible. Working memory will continue to be impaired. Prayer will still seem difficult. Anger will still make you want to punch people. And, shame will still creep into your life and destroy your self-esteem.

Lack of a Diagnosis Is a Headache, and In Some Cases, It Is Literally a Headache

As previously stated, not having an ADHD diagnosis can cause mental anguish and stress. When a person experiences a high amount of stress, their risk for a headache is increased. A 2014 study[ix] found that adolescents who felt they had an undiagnosed case of ADHD and/or learning disabilities experienced significantly more headaches than their peers who had been diagnosed. The risks of not getting a diagnosis are grim. If there is a suspicion of ADHD, it is imperative to see a mental health professional for a diagnosis.

Hidden Symptoms

The symptoms of ADHD can sometimes be masked or go unnoticed. A person of high intelligence can perform so well in school that they are seen as too high functioning to have ADHD,[59] and under the right circumstances, a person with ADHD can thrive. The symptoms can be hidden by well-developed coping strategies. If a person with ADHD can find ways of dealing with the symptoms of ADHD before seeking a diagnosis, there may be no noticeable signs of ADHD until those coping strategies break down.

This is why many diagnoses do not occur until the ADHDer goes to college. Once a student is away from their parents, the good habits previously enforced by parental mandate become optional. There is no one to ensure that homework gets done or that the student gets out of bed in the morning. Many college students find it hard to function without the structures that were in place during their years of living in their parents' house and attending a school where they moved from one class to the next all day. The lack of structures destroys the coping mechanisms that allowed the ADHD to go unnoticed.

---

59   That will not stop some people from telling them they are underachieving and need to try harder. That was the case for me until I sought a diagnosis.

This highlights why it is crucial to seek an ADHD diagnosis, even if you are not completely convinced you have ADHD. There may be subtle signs that you do have ADHD that are being overlooked. Examine those areas of your life where you work like crazy to meet deadlines or stay on top of a project or where you make a bunch of lists just to ensure you do not forget anything. Try to remember how often you have been told you are not reaching your full potential. Yes, you might waste a few afternoons only to find out that you do not have ADHD, but that is better than spending many years failing to reach your full potential.

Whom to See for a Diagnosis

The sad reality is many areas are woefully inadequate when it comes to diagnosing and treating ADHD. This makes it challenging to find a proper healthcare professional to meet your needs. Ideally, one should go to someone who specializes in ADHD. These people can be found on websites such as CHADD.org, ADDitudemag. com, add.org, or other websites that cater to those with ADHD. However, if there is no ADHD specialist in your geographic area (or insurance network), look for healthcare professionals who work in the mental health field (Psychiatrists, psychologists, therapists, etc.). Even if you are an adult, a child psychiatrist might be better than a psychiatrist who works with adults and/or people of all ages. Child psychiatrists are going to be more familiar with ADHD than those who do not specialize in child psychiatry. Patients with ADHD make up a higher percentage of a child psychiatrist's patients than is the case for other psychiatrists. While it is true a general practice doctor or a pediatrician can diagnose ADHD, they should be used as a last resort.[60] Your primary care physician simply does not have the expertise needed for the proper diagnosis and treatment of ADHD. This is especially true when it comes to medication. The process for finding the right medication for an ADHD patient is complicated, and unless the doctor knows what he/she is doing, it will almost certainly have dire consequences for the patient. A general practitioner could see that a child cannot behave and/or concentrate in school and simply give the child the same medication he does to every child with suspected ADHD. Additionally, a family practice physician does not have the requisite skills for identifying and differentiating between ADHD and conditions that can co-occur with ADHD. For best results, do your research and find the best mental health practitioner available to you.

WARNING

The process of getting an ADHD diagnosis is not pleasant. It is long, uncomfortable, and at times, incredibly frustrating.[61] That does not mean you should not go through the process. I just wanted you to be aware of what lies ahead in the diagnosis process and not be surprised like I was.

---

60   It is entirely possible some primary care physicians do know a great deal about ADHD and could provide better treatment than some psychiatrists. However, as a general rule, that is not the case.

61   One of the things I had to endure during my diagnosis process was playing a game with the lady administering the test. She did not explain the rules to me, and when I started to figure out the rules, she changed them on me. At least, I think she did. When I accused her of this, she neither confirmed nor denied that she was doing so.

Signs You Might Have ADHD

Below are some questions that are important to consider if you think that you or someone you know might have ADHD: [62]

1.) Do you constantly find yourself running late?

2.) Do you find time management impossible?

3.) Do you often speak without thinking?

4.) Does your inability to concentrate cause you emotional distress?

5.) Do you abhor boredom?

6.) Are you short-tempered?

7.) Do you frequently have creative or ingenuitive ideas?

8.) Do you frequently fidget?

10.) Do you feel like your successes in life happened by accident rather than by your hard work?

11.) Do you rely on caffeine to function?

12.) When telling a story, do you frequently go off on tangents?

13.) Do you frequently procrastinate?

14.) Do you frequently drive above the speed limit?

15.) Do you seek out dangerous activities or hobbies, such as skydiving, automobile racing, rock climbing, etc.?

16.) Do you make more careless mistakes than others?

17.) Did/Do you struggle in school?

18.) Do impending deadlines inspire a flurry of activity on your part?

19.) Does someone in your family have ADHD?

20.) Do you frequently feel out of place?

21.) Do you feel as though people do not understand you?

22.) Do you struggle to "fit in?"

23.) Do you make comments or jokes that others find odd or strange?

24.) In social situations, do you often say the wrong thing?

25.) Do you frequently change your hobbies?

26.) Are career or job changes common for you?

27.) Do people constantly tell you to try harder?

28.) In school, were you frequently in trouble?

29.) Have you ever broken the law?

29.) Do you have trouble with delayed gratification?

---

62   I adapted these question from a longer list in Doctors Edward Hallowell John Ratey's book *Delivered from Distraction*. I changed most of the questions to be more suitable to my liking, and I eliminated some questions altogether. I also added some of my own.

30.) Do you feel your thoughts race around your brain so fast that you cannot slow them down and deal with them one at a time?

31.) Do you ever get stuck down internet rabbit holes?

32.) Do you have a poor working memory?

33.) Do you have an excellent long-term memory?

34.) Do you ever become so engrossed in a task it is difficult to pull yourself away from it when it is time to move on to something else?

35.) Do you get restless when sitting for long periods of time?

36.) Do you struggle to get out of bed in the morning?

37.) Do you feel as though you cannot shut your brain off and go to sleep?

38.) Are you short-tempered?

39.) Have you frequently chosen poorly when selecting a romantic partner?

40.) Do you often finish reading an entire page of text and have no clue what you just read?

41.) Do you ever open an internet browser and find yourself unable to remember what you were going to look up?

42.) When you pick up your phone, do you ever forget what you were going to do with your phone because notifications distracted you?

43.) Have you ever had to delete an app from your smartphone or tablet because you wasted too much time on it?

44.) Is your home or workspace constantly a mess?

45.) Do you prefer listening to an audiobook over reading a book?

46.) Are you easily frustrated?

47.) Are you accident prone?

48.) As a child, were you a bed wetter?

49.) Do you still wet the bed?

50.) Do you feel like an underachiever?

51.) Have you found unique ways of coping with any of the problems listed above?

52.) Have you been thinking about several different topics while working through these questions?

53.) Did you pick up this book for the first time and immediately go to this chapter?

54.) Did you completely miss the fact there was no question #9?

55.) Did you completely miss the fact that there were two #29's?

56.) Did you fail to notice #6 and #38 were the same question?

57.) Have any of the above questions made you laugh?

58.) Have any of these questions made you uncomfortable?

59.) Do you feel like the person who wrote these questions knows you?

If you answered yes to most of the questions above, there is a chance you have ADHD. If you answered yes to almost all of the questions above, then there is a strong chance you have ADHD.

Note: These questions are not an exhaustive diagnostic tool. Only a trained professional can accurately diagnose ADHD.

Wait, I Came Here For Someone Else, But That Sounds a Lot Like Me

One of the stranger facts about ADHD[63] is that many times a person is not diagnosed with ADHD until their child is. During the process of learning about their child's newly diagnosed ADHD, a parent will often recognize some of their own struggles listed among the symptoms of ADHD. This leads to a conversation with their child's doctor, and soon, the parent has stumbled onto an ADHD diagnosis of their own. This is actually quite common. If your sibling has ADHD, there is a 25% chance that you have it as well, and if it is your child that has ADHD, there is 50% chance you have it, too.[64]

---

63   And, there are plenty of strange facts about ADHD!

64   Genetics…FUN FACT: Gregor Mendel, the father of genetics, was an Augustinian friar.

PART TWO:
FALLING

A CROSS, NOT A SUPERPOWER

"If anyone wishes to come after Me, he must deny himself and take up his cross daily and follow Me." – Luke 9:23

The ADHD Disadvantage

In recent years, there has been a movement within the ADHD community to re-brand ADHD as a sort of superpower. Yes, people who have ADHD can do great things, but it cannot be ignored that they have to overcome many challenges to become successful. In overcoming those challenges, those with ADHD need medication and many methods of coping and strategizing. Hyperfocus[65] can be beneficial if one hyperfocuses on something important, but when the object of the hyperfocus is not an important task, it can distract a person from what they should be doing. If I had the opportunity to choose a superpower for myself, I certainly would not choose ADHD.[66] Furthermore, I do not want to owe my achievements to a superpower. I want my achievements to be something I achieved through hard work. Moreover, I appreciate how struggling with ADHD has shaped who I am. As G.K. Chesterton once said, "Do not free a camel of the burden of his hump; you may free him from being a camel." Without enduring the struggles that come with ADHD, I would be a different person. I feel struggling with ADHD has helped me develop some resilient character traits. To characterize ADHD as a superpower would diminish or completely remove that part of me that is able to overcome challenges.

Society seems to be forcing an ideology upon us: Life should be easy. Anything that hurts you is bad and should not be embraced. If it feels good, do it. If it gets too difficult, give up and try something else. Pain and suffering is the enemy. Life should be worry-free. Anyone who tells you differently is a bigot and should be shunned. These are all lies.

Why ignore reality? Living with ADHD is challenging. There is no shame in stating that it is a burden. To acknowledge that it is a burden is to deny the feel-good ideology, and that seems to be the only sin society will acknowledge. If a person wants to follow Jesus' command to pick up their cross, the Bible says they can expect mockery.[67]

The number of sufferings a person with ADHD has to endure is not easy. Aside from the issues with executive functions discussed in the chapter "What is ADHD?", those with ADHD have to face emotional and spiritual difficulties as well.

---

65   Hyperfocus is explained in the chapter "What is ADHD?"

66   For the record, I would choose teleportation. It would greatly improve my punctuality and allow me to eat at my favorite restaurant more than once per year.

67   One is reminded of the scene in Mel Gibson's The Passion of the Christ when Jesus is given the Cross and one of the two men with whom He was crucified calls Him a fool for embracing His Cross.

However, There Is Nothing Wrong with You

It is easy to see the cross of having ADHD as something wrong with you. God wired your brain differently on purpose. You and I struggle with ADHD, but everyone else has something different about them that is a cross for them. There is a specific purpose behind every part of the way God created you.

Moreover, ADHD is a cross because the way the world operates is geared towards neurotypicals. To those who are wired differently, life is difficult because we are not the norm. If everyone had ADHD life would be easier because people would give us a list of instructions (rather than orally tell you twenty different things to do and expect you to remember them all), expect everyone to show up late, and struggle with the same things those of us with ADHD struggle to do.

Embrace Church Teaching, and Embrace Your Cross

By accepting ADHD as a cross and carrying that cross, we open ourselves up to uniting our sufferings with Christ's sufferings. This gives us the chance to encounter Christ in a unique and powerful way. Carrying the cross of ADHD is not easy, but we must always keep in mind our heavenly goal. In The Spiritual Exercises, Saint Ignatius of Loyola writes:

> Man is created to praise, reverence, and serve God our Lord, and by this means to save his soul.
>
> And the other things on the face of the earth are created for man and that they may help him in prosecuting the end for which he is created.
>
> From this it follows that man is to use them as much as they help him on to his end, and ought to rid himself of them so far as they hinder him as to it.
>
> For this it is necessary to make ourselves indifferent to all created things in all that is allowed to the choice of our free will and is not prohibited to it; so that, on our part, we want not health rather than sickness, riches rather than poverty, honor rather than dishonor, long rather than short life, and so in all the rest; desiring and choosing only what is most conducive for us to the end for which we are created.

What this means for those of us who have ADHD is that we are not to prefer having a neurotypical brain to having an ADHD brain. We should prefer the brain God gave us, for He gave us our brain for our sanctification. We were created for Him, and we ought to choose what will bring us closer to Him. Therefore, we are to embrace the gift of the cross of ADHD.

UNWANTED TAG-ALONGS

"Dogs surround me; a pack of evildoers closes in on me. They have pierced my hands and my feet I can count all my bones. They stare at me and gloat; they divide my garments among them; for my clothing they cast lots. But You, LORD, do not stay far off; my strength, come quickly to help me. Deliver my soul from the sword, my life from the grip of the dog. Save me from the lion's mouth, my poor life from the horns of wild bulls." – Psalm 22:17-22

Not ADHD Alone

Most people with ADHD have a comorbid condition. This means, along with ADHD, the individual has another mental health condition with which to cope. A Danish study[x] of individuals from age four to seventeen found that 52% of those with ADHD have a comorbid condition, and 26.2% had more than one comorbid condition.

The co-occurrence of ADHD and another condition makes the diagnosis and treatment of ADHD difficult. When symptoms of more than one mental health condition are present, it can be difficult to identify what exactly is going on with the patient's mental health. In these instances, mental health practitioners try to find out what conditions are present and whether the conditions present are co-occurring or if one condition is causing another. The existence of comorbid conditions complicates the patient's treatment. The healthcare provider has to determine if the conditions should be treated at the same time or if one should be addressed before the other. The DSM-V does offer some guidelines as to treatment priorities, but the answer is not always clear.

Anxiety

According to the American Psychological Association, "Anxiety is an emotion characterized by feelings of tension, worried thoughts and physical changes like increased blood pressure." Those with anxiety disorders have to deal with unwanted and intrusive thoughts that cause fear and worry. These feelings may cause those with anxiety disorders to avoid certain situations and to exhibit physiological symptoms such as sweating, trembling, dizziness, and an elevated heartbeat. Both anxiety disorders and ADHD cause inattention and restlessness, but the cause of these symptoms in anxiety is due to worry, which is not the case in ADHD. There are many anxiety disorders, and nearly half of adults with ADHD (47.1%) have an anxiety disorder of some sort[xi].

Generalized anxiety disorder (GAD) affects 8% of adults with ADHD.[xii] GAD is an anxiety disorder characterized by an excessive worry about a variety of topics.[xiii] To be diagnosed with GAD, a person must experience three GAD symptoms on more days than not for a period of over six months. These symptoms include restlessness or feeling keyed up or on edge, easily fatigued, difficulty concentrating or mind going blank, irritability, muscle tension, and sleep difficulties.[xiv]

Obsessive-compulsive disorder (OCD) can be found in 2.7% of adults with ADHD.[xv] One-third of children with obsessive compulsive disorder also have ADHD[xvi] Obsessive-compulsive disorder, like ADHD, is often misunderstood and cartooned in the media. The key to understanding OCD is the letter D, which stands for disorder. Obsessive-compulsive disorder is just that—a disorder. If you make fun of someone for being finicky about some things by saying they have OCD, please stop doing so. It is a disorder that causes serious problems. As defined by the International OCD Foundation, obsessive-compulsive disorder is "when a person gets caught in a cycle of obsessions and compulsions." For someone to be given an OCD diagnosis, their life must be severely hampered and disrupted by their obsessions and compulsions, and they must persist over a long period of time.[68] These obsessions are unwanted thoughts that invade the mind and refuse to leave, and compulsions are the actions a person takes to remove the obsessions.

Post-traumatic stress disorder (PTSD) affects 11.9% of adults with ADHD.[xvii] PTSD is an anxiety disorder brought on by a traumatic event. A person undergoes a traumatic event and is then plagued by anxiety because of the memory of that event. According to the National Institute of Mental Health, symptoms usually appear within three months of the event. There are four diagnostic criteria for PTSD:

• Re-experiencing symptoms such as flashbacks, nightmares, and frightening thoughts

• Avoiding people, places, objects, events, thoughts, or feelings that will remind a person of the traumatic event

• Symptoms related to arousal and reaction such as being easily startled, feeling on edge, difficulty sleeping, and outbursts of anger

• Issues with cognition and mood such as memory loss with regard to major parts of the traumatic event, negative thoughts about self or the world, unwarranted feelings of guilt and shame, and loss of interest in favorite activities.

Just over 29% of adults with ADHD have social anxiety disorder, also known as social phobia.[xviii] Social anxiety disorder (SAD) causes feelings of anxiety, fear, self-consciousness and embarrassment in normal daily social interactions.[xix] These feelings are stirred up because the person with SAD fears the scrutiny and judgment of others.

Autism Spectrum Disorders

Autism spectrum disorders are a group of developmental disorders that include a wide range of symptoms and levels of disabilities. These disorders are characterized by ongoing social and communication problems, repetitive behavior, limited interests, and other symptoms that interfere with a person's ability to function socially.[xx] Prior to the publication of the fifth edition of the Diagnostic and Statistical Manual of Mental Disorders (DSM-V), there were four separate autism spectrum disorders: Autistic disorder, Asperger's syndrome, childhood disintegrative disorder, and pervasive developmental disorder not otherwise specified.

---

68   Similar to how a person does not "get a little ADHD once in a while," a person does not "get a little OCD from time to time."

When distinguishing between ADHD and autism spectrum disorder, one must look at the social activity of the individual. Those with ADHD exhibit social dysfunction and peer rejection; whereas, those with autism spectrum disorder disengage socially, isolate themselves, and express indifference to facial and tonal communication cues from others. Both children with ADHD and autism spectrum disorder are prone to tantrums. However, those with ADHD throw tantrums because of impulsivity and self-control issues, and those with autism spectrum disorder display tantrums because they struggle to tolerate change in their life.

The DSM-IV had stated that those with an autism spectrum disorder could not be diagnosed with ADHD, but the DSM-V changed that. Now, it is possible to be diagnosed with both an autism spectrum disorder and ADHD. In fact, the DSM-V goes so far as to state that "[w]hen criteria for both ADHD and autism spectrum disorder are met, both diagnoses should be given."

However, the DSM-V was only published in 2013, which limits the amount of research that is available on the comorbidity of autism spectrum disorders and ADHD. A 2013 study published by the American Academy of Pediatrics found that 18% of children with ADHD exhibited autistic traits.[xxi] Another study, published before the publication of the DSM-V, found that 30-50% of those with autism spectrum disorder exhibited symptoms of ADHD. The previously mentioned Danish study found that 12.4% of ADHD patients have an autism spectrum disorder.[xxii]

Conduct Disorder

According to the DSM-V, conduct disorder is characterized by aggression towards people and animals, destruction of property, deceit, theft, and serious violation of rules.[69] These symptoms can have their onset in childhood or adolescence. Furthermore, conduct disorder can also be intensified by a presentation with limited prosocial emotions (e.g. callousness, lack of remorse, etc.). Moreover, a 2011 study[xxiv] found that boys with ADHD and conduct disorder displayed a higher risk for delinquency than controls. A 2006 study in Europe found that 46% of children with ADHD also had conduct disorder.[xxv]

Developmental Coordination Disorder

Developmental coordination disorder (DCD), also known as dyspraxia, is a condition that affects a child's ability to develop motor skills properly. These children are often described as "clumsy" by parents and teachers. It is quite common for those with ADHD to be accident-prone. In fact, according to CanChild, an organization headquartered in McMaster University's School of Rehabilitation Science, half of children who are diagnosed with ADHD receive a diagnosis of DCD.

---

69   The DSM-V goes into much more detail on these characteristics and lists multiple symptoms within each category.

Enuresis

Enuresis is involuntary urination. This condition is not limited to children; adults can and do suffer from enuresis. Although, enuresis is mostly found in children. For most individuals, potty training removes the possibility of involuntary urination, but for some, this problem does not go away or returns. This happens not only at night but also during the day.

It is important to distinguish, then, between nocturnal enuresis and diurnal enuresis. Nocturnal enuresis is bedwetting at night. Those who suffer from nocturnal enuresis are most often heavy sleepers and do not wake up properly when the bladder is full. These individuals do not get the message from the brain that there is a need to wake up and eliminate urine until it is too late. In these cases, cognitive behavioral therapy has been known to be effective in treating enuresis.[70] Diurnal enuresis is wetting one's pants during the day. Both problems are frustrating for parents and embarrassing for children.

Another distinction that needs to be made is the one between primary enuresis and secondary enuresis. Primary enuresis is the most common form and occurs in children who have never successfully established control over their bladder for longer than six months. Secondary enuresis occurs in children who have been able to establish control over their bladders successfully and have been able to control their bladder for more than six months. In the case of secondary enuresis, the resumption of involuntary urination is often the result of stress from familial, social, or school-related sources.

Studies have demonstrated the strong connection between ADHD and enuresis[xxvi] and that ADHD can increase the likelihood of persistent enuresis.[xxvii] One study of six-year-olds found that children with ADHD are 2.7 times more likely to have nocturnal enuresis and 4.5 times more likely to have diurnal enuresis than peers.[xxviii]

Impulse Control Disorders

One of the symptoms of ADHD is impulsivity. It is, therefore, not surprising that those with ADHD are prone to having a comorbid disorder that affects their impulsivity. Nearly 20% of adults with ADHD have an impulse control disorder called intermittent explosive disorder (IED).[xxix] In intermittent explosive disorder, a person is prone to outbursts of anger and violence that are not justified by the situation. Those with IED show serious aggression towards others, a characteristic not present in those with ADHD.

Migraines

There is emerging research that suggests that those with ADHD are prone to having migraines. A 2011 study[xxx] found that adults with ADHD, both males and females, suffer migraines at a higher rate than a control group made up of individuals who do not have ADHD.

Migraines are extraordinarily painful headaches that are usually confined to one side of the head and accompanied

---

70   For example, special alarms can be purchased that goes off to alert the individual suffering from enuresis that they need to wake up and use the toilet.

by nausea, vomiting, and sensitivity to light and sound.[xxxi] For many, migraines are reoccurring and can last for hours or days. The cause of migraines is unknown.

Mood Disorders

ADHDers are likely to have a comorbid mood disorder. It has been reported that mood disorders affect 38.3% of those with ADHD.[xxxii] Mood disorders cause disturbances in a person's emotional state that are not considered normal. There are two main categories of mood disorders: bipolar disorders and depressive disorders.

Bipolar disorders affect 19.4% of adults with ADHD.[xxxiii] This group of disorders features extreme mood changes. These mood changes can take the form of manic episodes where a person is either abnormally high-spirited or irritable, hypomanic episodes which are less severe manic episodes, and major depressive episodes where a person exhibits many of the symptoms of major depressive disorder. There are three main types of bipolar disorders, bipolar I disorder, bipolar II disorder, and cyclothymic disorder. To be diagnosed with bipolar I, a person must have suffered a manic episode that may be preceded or followed by hypomanic or major depressive episodes.[xxxiv] In bipolar II disorder, a person has suffered at least one hypomanic episode and at least one major depressive episode but not a manic episode.[xxxv] A person can be diagnosed with cyclothymic disorder when they have experienced periods of hypomanic symptoms and depressive symptoms (but less severe than major depression) for two years or one year in the case of children and teens.[xxxvi] Both ADHD and bipolar disorder can cause similar inattentive symptoms and moods expressed in the extreme. However, the moods caused by ADHD can change several times per day, and those caused by bipolar disorder last for several days at a time.

It has been reported that 18.6% of adults with ADHD have major depressive disorder.[xxxvii] Among children, 6-30% of ADHD patients have major depression.[xxxviii] This disorder is what most people think of when they think of depression. Symptoms caused by major depressive disorder include feeling sad, feeling hopeless, anger and frustration over small things, irritability, loss of interest in favorite activities, too much or too little sleep, lack of energy, increased or decreased appetite resulting in weight gain or loss, anxiety, restlessness, guilt over past actions, feelings of worthlessness or guilt, decreased mental faculties, unexplained physical ailments, and frequent thoughts of death and suicide. Those with depression will also suffer from inattention. However, the inattention only surfaces during depressive episodes.

A study found that 12.8% of adults with ADHD have dysthymia,[xxxix] a milder but more long-term form of depression. Also known as dysthymic disorder or persistent depression disorder, dysthymia causes a lot of the same symptoms as major depressive disorder such as loss of interest in normal activities, sadness, feeling down, hopelessness, lack of energy, low self-esteem, trouble concentrating, trouble making decisions, irritability, excessive anger, decreased activity and productivity, avoidance of social activities, feeling guilty about the past, poor appetite or overeating, and sleep problems.

Oppositional Defiant Disorder

The Mayo Clinic defines oppositional defiant disorder as "a frequent and persistent pattern of anger, irritability, arguing, defiance or vindictiveness toward [parents] and other authority figures." This definition makes it hard to distinguish between ODD and the tantrums any child will throw. The DSM-V dictates that, in order for a person to be diagnosed with oppositional defiant disorder, they must exhibit ODD for at least six months. This behavior is defined by the exhibition of four of eight criteria that are found within three categories: angry/irritable mood, argumentative/defiant behavior, or vindictiveness.

An ODD outburst has been described as a chemical freight train. In essence, the person suffering from ODD is being held captive by external stimuli during the outburst. It is important for parents of children with ODD to know that these outbursts are not personal. Without proper treatment for ODD (which often includes medication), the individual is powerless to control these outbursts.

A 2006 European study[xl] found that 67% of children with ADHD had oppositional defiant disorder. Another estimate states that oppositional defiant disorder occurs in 25-75% of children with ADHD. Additionally, a 2011 study[xlii] also found that boys with both ADHD and ODD displayed a higher risk for delinquency than controls, but not as high of a risk as those with ADHD and conduct disorder.

There is some difficulty in diagnosing a child who has ADHD with ODD, however. This is because some individuals with ADHD will develop a strong negative attitude towards the school work or other activities that require sustained mental effort. The symptoms of ODD must not be related to disliking tasks a person with ADHD struggles to accomplish.

Sensory Processing Disorder

Sensory processing disorder is when a person does not properly handle, process, and act upon various external sensory information. Persons suffering from this condition will over-respond or under-respond to various stimuli. For example, one might cover one's ears in loud environments, find many items of clothing itchy, or show little to no reaction to pain.

This condition receives varied acceptance in the mental health field. Those who do not accept sensory processing disorder point out that sensory processing issues could be caused by conditions such as anxiety, autism, or ADHD and that there is insufficient evidence supporting its designation as a diagnosable condition. The DSM-V and the ICD-10[71] do not recognize it due to the lack of evidence. While not being listed in the DSM-V and the ICD-10, it is recognized in the Diagnostic Classification of Mental Health and Developmental Disorders of Infancy and Early Childhood-Revised. There are a number of stories from parents of children who have sensory processing issues that can be easily found by doing a Google search that make a strong case for its acceptance as a diagnosable

---

71   The international version of the DSM.

condition.[72]

Regardless of whether or not sensory processing disorder is a real condition, it has been widely noted that a significant number of children with ADHD do not have the normal capacity for processing external stimuli. Evidence of sensory processing disorder (also called sensory processing dysfunction, sensory processing deficits, and sensory modulation disorder) has been found more often in children with ADHD than in those who do not have ADHD.[xliii]

Sleep Difficulties

As discussed in other chapters, sleep is a significant issue for those with ADHD. Sleep-related problems caused by or are comorbid with ADHD have a later onset in the life course than do most ADHD symptoms. This made the link between ADHD and sleep difficult to understand. Therefore, only recently[73] have researchers begun to study the connection between ADHD and sleep difficulties.

Three problems are of particular interest when discussing ADHD and sleep problems: Insomnia, restless leg syndrome, and sleep-disordered breathing. Insomnia occurs when one has ample opportunity to sleep but is unable to fall or remain asleep. This leaves one feeling tired the next day and can cause the symptoms of ADHD to increase in severity. Restless leg syndrome describes the irresistible desire to move one's legs to relieve uncomfortable sensations while at rest. According to Children and Adults with Attention Deficit Hyperactivity Disorder (CHADD), up to 44% of those with ADHD might have restless leg syndrome. Sleep-disordered breathing describes a spectrum of issues from obstructive sleep apnea to primary snoring. According to CHADD, these sleep problems affect 25-30% of children with ADHD. Those with ADHD might also have a disordered circadian rhythm, which is when one's sleep patterns do not correspond with the time of day.

Specific Learning Disorder

According to CHADD, up to half of children with ADHD have a learning disability.[74] ADHD alone makes it challenging to achieve one's potential, but the addition of a learning disability increases the difficulties a child with ADHD will face in keeping up with their peers in school. It is important to note when inattention is symptomatic of specific learning disorder but not ADHD. Those with specific learning disorder do appear inattentive in class because learning is difficult for them, but they will be able to focus outside of school, though.

The two most common learning disabilities that can co-exist with ADHD are dyslexia and dyscalculia. According to the International Dyslexia Association, dyslexia is "a language-based learning disability characterized by difficulties with accurate and fluent word recognition, spelling, and reading decoding." Dyscalculia is similar to

---

72   Anecdotal evidence does not necessarily qualify it for scientific acceptance.

73   There was a time when sleep issues were a diagnostic criterion for ADHD, but it was eliminated because of how late the onset of the sleep issues was.

74   Other sources estimate the percentage of children with both ADHD and a learning disability could be as high as 60%.

dyslexia, but instead of having issues with language and words, those with dyscalculia have difficulties understanding mathematical concepts. Glynis Hannell, a psychologist and the author of Dyscalculia: Action Plans for Successful Learning in Mathematics, states that dyscalculia occurs in about 20% of students with ADHD.

Learning disabilities in those with ADHD are not limited to language and mathematical problems. A third learning disability can affect writing skills. This is known as dysgraphia which is characterized by difficulty holding writing utensils, poor handwriting, grammar and spelling errors, easily tired hands while writing, unable to express thoughts in writing, and incomplete writing assignments. Moreover, CHADD also points out that 12% of children with ADHD also have speech problems.

Other Issues

The comorbid conditions listed above are not all of the conditions that can co-exist with ADHD. Other problems plaguing ADHDers include but are not limited to eating disorders, Tourette's syndrome, and substance use disorder. Patients with ADHD are 1.82 times more likely to develop an eating disorder than those who do not have ADHD, and this propensity is more prevalent in girls.[xliv] ADHD and Tourette's syndrome co-occur 55% of the time[xlv]. Substance use disorder can be found in 15.2% of adults with ADHD,[xlvi] and half of adolescents with substance use disorder have ADHD.[xlvii]

EMOTIONAL STRUGGLES

"[W]e even boast of our afflictions, knowing that affliction produces endurance, and endurance, proven character, and proven character, hope, and hope does not disappoint, because the love of God has been poured out into our hearts through the holy Spirit that has been given to us." – Romans 5:3-5

MY EMOTIONS! MY EMOTIONS![75]

People with ADHD experience the same emotions people without ADHD experience. However, the regulation of emotions is a huge problem for those with ADHD, and those who do not have ADHD are much better at controlling their emotions. While emotional dysregulation is not included in the diagnostic criteria for ADHD, it is, nevertheless, common among those who suffer from ADHD. A 2012 study[xlviii] pointed out that "[e]mpirical studies have confirmed a high prevalence of this psychopathological feature [emotional dysregulation] in adults with ADHD that compares to the frequency of the ADHD core symptoms, inattention, hyperactivity and impulsivity."

ADHD brains are often overwhelmed by emotions, which impairs logical thinking.[76] When your brain works as fast as an ADHD brain does, it can be hard to slow thoughts that increase stress and emotional responses. The anterior cingulate cognitive division, a functional subdivision within the anterior cingulate cortex that is key in complex cognitive/attentional processing, has been found to be dysfunctional in adults with ADHD[xlix] and cause problems with emotional self-control.[l]

Moreover, ADHDers are passionate people. We are usually all-in or not-at-all; there is no gray area. Unfortunately, this means our emotions tend to be all-in. We have a tendency to feel all of the emotions when they arise. The struggles brought on by ADHD make us hypersensitive. For example, the correction of our errors, even when those errors are corrected charitably, can cause hurt feelings.

Rejection Sensitive Dysphoria

The intense emotions of ADHD can lead to extreme responses when an ADHDer is rejected or perceives that they are being rejected by someone close to them. This has been termed rejection sensitive dysphoria[li] (RSD) by Doctor William Dodson, an ADHD expert. People with ADHD who experience RSD[77] experience intense emotional responses to rejection, and they find it hard even to describe the intensity of their emotions. When those emotions remain internalized, these feeling can imitate the symptoms of major mood disorders. These symptoms can even escalate to suicide ideation. However, when the feelings are externalized, the result is an explosion of rage. RSD can

---

75   +10 points to anyone who caught the reference

76   Sometimes, I wish I was Spock.

77   According to Doctor Dodson, 98-99% of people with ADHD experience RSD.

also lead ADHDers to be hypervigilant about avoiding rejection because they expect to be rejected.

This is something I know all too well. When a friend has not spoken to me for a while, I begin to wonder why they do not like me anymore. In the calendar year 2018, I was dumped twice. Both breakups hit me quite hard. The first sent me into a painful emotional state for two months. The final day of that emotional downturn was spent thinking about what would be the most painless way of killing myself would be. Luckily, the next day, things turned around, and I began to heal. Then, I entered another relationship with another woman, and after about six months of that relationship, she, too, broke up with me. A few hours later, I found myself unable to stop identifying all of the things in my house that could be used as a noose. I then drove to a local mental health facility that does free mental health evaluations 24 hours per day. This is the extreme side of RSD,[78] but many ADHDers will relate to the strong emotions caused by rejection.

Anger

One of the emotions with which those with ADHD have to contend is anger. ADHDers have little patience. We want what we want now, not later. This leads to situations where we run out of patience and anger boils over. Angry outbursts are common with those with ADHD. We do not intend to lose our cool, but we do. It can take a long time for ADHDers to learn how to control our tempers. In describing this struggle to control anger and other emotions, Doctor Edward Hallowell, an expert in ADHD who has ADHD, says ADHDers have a Ferrari brain with bicycle brakes. Anger can intensify other problems ADHDers have. For example, when anger and impulsivity are combined, it can lead to people getting punched.

Failure

Allegedly smart and successful people like to talk about how failure is good and helps people learn. They might even go so far as to state that everyone fails and that everyone should fail. That may be true, but those with ADHD fail far more often than the average person. That takes a toll on us. The list of failures seems much longer than the list of successes. Instead of defining ourselves by our strengths, we find our failures to be better descriptors of ourselves. Encouragement from family, friends, and teachers ring hollow to us. They tell us we have so much potential, but we do not believe it.

Sooner or later, it becomes tempting to make failure our identity. This is a denial of reality. By ignoring our gifts, we deny the beauty of God's creation, of which we are an important part. We begin to hyperfocus on our mistakes, and they are all we think about. When we finally stop thinking about our failures, our future thoughts about ourselves are altered in a negative way. It creates a false perspective of oneself, and it is not easy to rid oneself of that perspective.

---

78   It should also be noted that my mental health struggles have been impacted by more than just these two breakups.

Delayed gratification is not a strong suit for ADHDers. If we sucked at managing our ADHD yesterday and we still suck today, it is upsetting. It is hard for us to recognize that we cannot instantly conquer ADHD or any other challenge in life. Improvement takes time. Not immediately seeing the fruit of our efforts to improve our lives can get extremely frustrating.[79] This only compounds the problems we have due to ADHD, especially our emotional struggles.

Overwhelmed

When too much is happening, ADHDers do not do well. In a room full of people and noises, it can be hard to tune out what is not necessary and focus on what is in front of us. At social gatherings, if too many conversations are happening at once, I am not able to concentrate on any of them.[80]

Too much information too fast can cause our ADHD brains to overload. Instead of remembering the information, we breakdown, and emotions flare up. This is even more dangerous when it is emotions and not information. In the moment, it is hard to recognize that it is okay to step away and take a break from the multitude of stimuli. In fact, we need to step away. No good can come from a conversation that is too emotionally charged. When a person with ADHD is feeling overwhelmed, one of the best things they can do is take a break.

Breaks are a necessity for those with ADHD. We need time to relax and have fun. It is tempting when we are constantly falling behind on tasks to think we need to work longer than others to get stuff done, but without time to relax and forget about our anxieties, we will lose control and sink into a negative mindset.

Unable to Enjoy Success

Yes, ADHDers like rewards. It is essential to getting the dopamine we crave. However, when we finish a project or find success in another area, we find it hard to enjoy our success. The challenge and the sense of determination we had in the face of that challenge have gone away. We are left missing the stimulus we received from the challenge.

We also are used to failing and being criticized. It can be surprising when things actually work out in our favor. We are never quite sure how we are supposed to handle success.[81] We might even try to downplay our success or feel like an imposter. This may sound strange to neurotypicals, but it is quite common for ADHDers.

---

79 Long-term goals? Ain't nobody got time for dat! (+10 points to anyone who caught the reference)

80 This is, however, preferable to having only one boring conversation.

81 I have found that, when a girl says yes to a second date (and especially when she says yes to even more dates), I find myself expecting her to eventually say, "Actually, could you stop talking to me."

Feeling Different

Many people who get diagnosed with ADHD later in life will report always feeling different growing up.[82] This makes it really hard to relate to others. We feel like no one understands our struggles, making it hard for us to reach out for help when our problems feel overwhelming.

By the way, everyone has something that makes them different. It is what makes humanity beautiful. When an ADHDer begins to feel bad about their differences, it is a tragedy because they have lost sight of the fact God had a plan when He was creating them, a plan for happiness, not woe.[83]

Misunderstood

While growing up and even into my young adulthood, I often felt like no understood me. Yes, sometimes ADHD can wreak havoc with my ability to express what I am thinking or feeling clearly, but I have often felt misunderstood on a deeper level. It stings when those I care about most do or say something that demonstrates that they do not understand me. If I have known someone for a long time or have grown close to someone, I expect them to know my quirks, eccentricities, and flaws and be understanding of them. Yet, too often, I find people I care about saying or doing something that they would not say or do if they truly knew me. Furthermore, if I have opened myself up to them and become vulnerable with them, I expect them to understand me. It is demoralizing when I discover that they do not.

Lack of Confidence

Because of all of the problems listed above, it can be hard for an ADHDer to feel confident. A high frequency of failure and difficulties making decisions leads one to lack confidence. We expect to fail. No matter how many times we have overcome our weaknesses, we continue to remember our past failures and allow them to dictate our expectations.

Furthermore, it can be difficult to stand up for oneself. Those with ADHD face constant criticism,[84] and it can be hard to refute those voices. Instead of letting others know when they have crossed a line, we take the abuse and allow others to continue lobbing bricks of criticism at our glass house of self-esteem.

No! What Are You Talking About? I Don't Have ADHD

When all you can think about are the negative aspects of having ADHD, it can be easy to accept the stigma ADHD carries. The stigma should not exist, but when we give in to self-deprecating thoughts, we perpetuate the stigma. We recognize ourselves in what others mistakenly think about ADHD, and shame creeps into our life.

---

82 I first read about this phenomenon while studying ADHD one day. When I read it, I had to stop myself from shouting, "That's me!"

83 See Jeremiah 29:11

84 Sometimes, the criticism comes from within.

SHAME

"I was at the point of death, my life was nearing the depths of Sheol; I turned every way, but there was no one to help; I looked for support but there was none. Then I remembered the mercies of the Lord, His acts of kindness through ages past; For He saves those who take refuge in Him, and rescues them from every evil. So I raised my voice from the grave; from the gates of Sheol I cried for help. I called out: Lord, You are my Father, my champion, my savior! Do not abandon me in time of trouble, in the midst of storms and dangers. I will always praise Your name and remember You in prayer! Then the Lord heard my voice, and listened to my appeal." – Sirach 51:6-11

My Struggle

Once again, I would like to revisit the story of how I became convinced I needed to see a healthcare professional about ADHD. Those daily visits to the Adoration chapel were less fruitful than I desired them to be due to my inattention. If I could not focus on prayer, allegedly the most important part of my life, how could I claim that I was taking my faith seriously? My lack of focus began to weigh on me, and one thought began to dominate my mind: What is wrong with me?

Before I got diagnosed with ADHD, the fact that I could not focus on prayer made me feel like crap. I love my faith. It is the most important aspect of my life. With an attitude like that, one would think that I could hyperfocus on prayer, but I cannot. It was (and still is) extremely frustrating to have an inability to focus while praying stunt my spiritual growth. I took my faith seriously, made a conscious effort to dress appropriately for Mass, went to daily Mass, Adoration, and Confession. Yet, whenever an old lady would approach me and say how much she appreciated my reverence,[85] I would feel like a fraud. I would think, *If you only knew how little I actually paid attention today...*

Negative Self-Talk

Those of us with ADHD often feel ashamed when our symptoms cause us difficulty in both our spiritual and everyday lives. We have heard so many criticisms about ourselves from others that we eventually internalize them and begin to criticize ourselves, making it easy to start believing we have less value than we actually do. When we are going to do something,[86] we hear a voice in the back of our heads telling us that we should give up because there is no way we could ever do that thing we are trying to do. In short, we become our own worst critic.

---

85   Despite how I make this seem, it is not all that common of an occurrence. Most often, if a little old lady stops me after Mass, she asks if I am a seminarian. When I say that I am not, the next question is, "Are you going to be a seminarian soon?" Following another "No," the question, "Have you ever thought of being a priest?" is asked. When I say that I have but God is not calling me to be a priest, she then says, "I'll pray for you," and gives me a look that says, "Oh, you are going to be a priest someday; you just don't know it yet." Then, I resist the urge to punch her in the back of the head as she walks away.

86   It could be anything!

It Is Going to Be Okay

When you struggle to pray, it can be easy to give in to the temptation to feel bad about yourself. *If prayer is important in the spiritual life and you are unable to pray, then you clearly must not want to improve in the spiritual life. You know you should strive to improve, but if you are not even paying attention, are you really trying?* As I write these words, it easy for me to see how quickly I can recreate all of the insecurities I have felt about my spiritual life and my lack of ability to focus on prayer,[87] These are the voices I have to ignore on a daily basis, as I find myself planning my next meal instead of listening to a homily or meditating on the mysteries of the Rosary.

There is something to which I keep returning whenever shame tries to re-enter my life. I remind myself that I am who God made me to be. If God did not want me to struggle with ADHD, He would not have allowed me to have ADHD. If He allowed it, there must be some way I can grow from it. If you are experiencing what I have experienced in my life because of ADHD, feel no shame. You are who God intended you to be.

To Confess or Not to Confess? That Is the Question.

Before we go any further, I want to make it clear that I am neither a theologian nor a canon lawyer. What follows is my opinion and should not be taken as an explanation of Church teaching.

The topic of feeling bad about the inability to focus during prayer raises an interesting question: Do I need to confess not paying attention during prayer? Does ADHD mitigate guilt assigned to the wanderings of the mind during prayer?

"How much is ADHD to blame for my distractions, and how much am I responsible?" is a debate I have every time I go to Confession or any time I examine my conscience. I am not looking for a free pass or an excuse to not pay attention. I want to pay attention, but I know I have my struggles. I want to know when I have done something wrong and when I was simply a victim of ADHD.

Furthermore, another difficulty with determining whether or not to confess a lack of focus during prayer is knowing what is normal. From what I have been told, it would seem everyone suffers from some level of distraction in prayer. Just how much are normal[88] people distracted? This makes it hard to know where we should be with our focus and how to describe to our confessors our struggles with attention,[89] I have never known what normal is. How do I know when I am at a normal level of focus?

The best advice a priest has ever given me on this debate is to examine whether or not I have given into my distractions,[90] In other words, when I realize I am thinking about something other than prayer, do I continue to think

---

87   I am even tempted to stop writing this. It is hard to discuss.

88   I use normal to refer to non-ADHDers. Who among us actually is normal?

89   Or our doctors! Am I the only one who does not know if I am adequately being treated for ADHD? Have I achieved as close to normal as I can expect? These are the things about which I think…

90   Shout out to Father Jordan Samson! #baller

about that thing, or do I try to return to prayer?[91] That has sort of helped me with figuring out what to do. It is hard to know, though, if I have consented to another, almost immediate, distracted thought.

Ignore the Shame

Through the amazing Sacrament of Reconciliation, we can receive forgiveness for our sins. There is no need to dwell on the shame. Our desire to grow closer to the Lord is the key. Focus on that. When distractions come, bring yourself back to prayer as soon as you notice your attention has gone elsewhere. The words of Saint Francis de Sales remind us of the unique opportunity turning back to the Lord in prayer can bring:

If the heart wanders or is distracted, bring it back to the point quite gently and replace it tenderly in its Master's presence. And even if you did nothing during the whole of your hour but bring your heart back and place it again in Our Lord's presence, though it went away every time you brought it back, your hour would be very well employed.

91　However, deciding to stop thinking about a distraction is a lot like saying, "Don't think about elephants." You end up thinking about what you said you were going to ignore.

TRUST

"My grace is sufficient for you, for power is made perfect in weakness." — 2 Corinthians 12:9

My Biggest Struggle

We now come to the chapter I had no clue how to write but knew needed to be included in this book—the chapter on trust. I almost did not include this chapter in this book because trust is probably the biggest struggle I have in my relationship with God, and I had no idea what I was going to say on the topic. For most of my life, my trust in God was minimal at best. I know trusting in the Lord is a crucial aspect of being a disciple, but following through on that knowledge has been far from easy.[92] Only in the past few years have I felt my trust in the Lord begin to increase[93]. How does one begin to write about trusting God when one knows so little about it?

When We Hit a Wall

What do we do when we discover that we cannot do it on our own? Even when we think we are relying on God to help us, we can still find ourselves stuck and unable to progress in the spiritual life. We have come face to face with our limitations, and this can be frustrating. There is nothing we can do, but we know we must move forward. In these moments, do we feel worthless, or do we turn to the Lord?

I once brought feelings of shame into the confessional and told the priest of my struggles with ADHD and how I was giving into self-deprecating thoughts. For my penance, the priest instructed me to meditate on the scripture verse at the beginning of this chapter and surrender my limitations to the Lord. In my meditation, an image appeared in my mind. I was walking and literally hit a brick wall. I looked to my left and my right, and there seemed to be no end to this wall. I looked up. The wall was too high to jump over, and there was nothing I could hold onto as I climbed the wall. I was stuck. I looked up once more and saw a beautiful, bright light shining down. As I continued staring at this light, a bucket (like one might find in an old well) was lowered down to me. It did not look like this rickety, old bucket and the rope to which it was attached could hold me, but I stepped into the bucket. I was then lifted up towards the light.

How Do We Grow in Trust?

I have wrestled with the question of how to grow in trust for a long time, and I have yet to find a satisfying answer to that question. There is no switch one can flip to automatically trust God more. The only answer I can

---

92   To put it mildly

93   Which is odd because I feel like the most amount of uncertainty I have had about my life and my future has occurred over the past few years

provide is the example of my own life.

As I mentioned above, my level of trust in God throughout my life has been low. However, after years of begging God to grant me the grace of trust in Him, I have felt my trust in Him start to grow. If anyone can learn anything from that pitiful story, it is that prayer works. I asked for God to help me trust Him, and He did. It took me pestering Him a bunch for it to happen, but it eventually worked. As Saint Eugène de Mazenod once said, "Don't be afraid to be importunate;[94] God is rich and generous enough to satisfy everyone."

---

94   Importunate, a great word to have in one's vocabulary, means persistent to the point of being annoying.

PRAYER (OR LACK THEREOF)

"In the same way, the Spirit too comes to the aid of our weakness; for we do not know how to pray as we ought, but the Spirit itself intercedes with inexpressible groanings." – Romans 8:26

Prayer: The Great Mystery

Take a moment and think about prayer. You know what it is. Or, do you? Quick, take out a piece of paper and a writing utensil, or save a tree and write in a note-taking app on your phone. Using your own words and ideas, write a definition of the word "prayer." Not easy, is it? I have spent almost all of my life figuring out what prayer is and have been unable to find a satisfying answer.

My favorite definition of prayer comes from Saint Thérèse: "For me, prayer is a surge of the heart." When all else fails, give God your heart. Let Him know what is going on in your life.

Another definition I like comes from Saint Eugène de Mazenod. He said, "[Prayer] is the furnace to which one comes to draw fire from the divine love." Prayer has a benefit. We receive from God in prayer. Some people refer to prayer as a conversation, but that has never quite felt right to me. In my mind, a conversation involves speaking to others using words. God rarely speaks using audible words. He communicates through the heart. Prayer is not the communication of words but the communication of hearts.

Is It Possible to Pray When You Have ADHD?

Theoretically speaking, it is, in fact, possible to pray when one has ADHD. I will be the first to admit that it is not easy to pray when you have ADHD, but that does not mean we should give up. Everyone needs to pray, no matter our limitations.

It is important to remember that God accepts us as we are. If all we can muster is a short, little prayer, that is what will please God most. We are to pray as we can, not as we think we should.[95] If you are just beginning praying, do not take up a daily holy hour or a 54-day Rosary novena[96]. Start with something you know you can do, and increase it from there.

One of the best moments of my spiritual life is when I realized that prayer does not need to be grand. God wants our brokenness offered up to Him. One of the best prayers, in my opinion, is only two words long: "Lord,

---

95   As we say in the coaching world, don't should yourself.

96   Can we stop calling 54-days of a specific prayer a novena? Novena means nine, not 54.

help."[97] I know a woman who also has ADHD and for years could only pray three prayers: "Good morning, God," "This day is Yours. Take control of my life beginning today," and "Thank You. Goodnight, God." Simple? Yes. Elegant? No. Pleasing to God? Absolutely. Do not forget the parable Jesus told of the Pharisee and the tax collector:[lii]

Two people went up to the temple area to pray; one was a Pharisee and the other was a tax collector. The Pharisee took up his position and spoke this prayer to himself, "O God, I thank you that I am not like the rest of humanity—greedy, dishonest, adulterous—or even like this tax collector. I fast twice a week, and I pay tithes on my whole income." But the tax collector stood off at a distance and would not even raise his eyes to heaven but beat his breast and prayed, "O God, be merciful to me a sinner." I tell you, the latter went home justified, not the former; for everyone who exalts himself will be humbled, and the one who humbles himself will be exalted.

Why worry about how one prays? Find what works for you and what you need out of prayer, and do it.

Transitioning into Prayer

Transitioning from one task to another is difficult when one has ADHD. So, when it comes to prayer or attending Mass, it can be hard to leave behind what one was doing just prior to entering into what is supposed to be a prayerful state. For example, when it is early, I use peppy music to wake myself up. Then, I find myself fighting off singing OMI's "Cheerleader" in my head during the Gospel. One helpful tip I often read on the internet and in books is to give oneself plenty of time in between tasks so as to have the time to mentally transition. Although, this can be difficult if one is constantly finding oneself running late.[98]

Is It Prayer, Or Is My Mind Just Wandering Aimlessly?[99]

People like to say that God makes use of our brokenness. It is possible that God can take our wandering thoughts and make them prayerful. I do believe God has spoken to me through my crazy ADHD trains of thought. This is the reason I like Lectio Divina.[100] It can create a situation where one uses one's imagination to enter into prayer. This is one of the most promising methods of prayer for those with ADHD. Lectio Divina has helped me make my wandering thoughts prayerful. I once had a powerful prayer experience while praying Lectio Divina with Luke 7:36-50 because I could not stop thinking about feet and how gross they are.

---

97   My physics teacher at the Catholic high school I attended led us in prayer before every class. On the day of a really tough test, this prayer was how we began the class period.

98   A common occurrence for people with ADHD. See the chapter entitled "MASSive Difficulties" for more on this.

99   In the interest of full disclosure, let me say that I do not have a legitimate answer to this question, but I am going to try my best to give you some things about which to think.

100   I explain what Lectio Divina is in the chapter entitled "Prayer Tips."

The Rosary

One of the selling points of the Rosary is that it only takes fifteen minutes to pray. It takes me thirty minutes to pray a Rosary. I never seem to be able to stay on track, and I often find myself starting prayers over because I lost where I was. They say you are supposed to meditate on the mysteries of the Rosary while you pray it, but I do not believe I have ever done that[101]. I think many others with ADHD will agree with me that it is a difficult method of prayer for us.

However, I can see where some with ADHD would love the Rosary. The opportunity to meditate on the mysteries of the Rosary could allow the imagination to run wild within the stories of the lives of Jesus and Mary. Plus, the Rosary is an object you hold while you pray. I quite often fiddle with the beads of my Rosary, making it kind of like a fidget toy.[102]

Minimal Spiritual Reading

Reading is problematic when you have ADHD. You can be reading through a page, but your mind is elsewhere. It is terribly frustrating to get to the end of a page and discover that you have absolutely no idea what you just read. You are left with two options: Start the page over or give up. In short, reading comprehension is a challenge for those with ADHD. This makes spiritual reading (e.g. reading books written by popes, saints, Scott Hahn, etc.) next to impossible.

Almost all experts on Catholic spirituality agree that one of the keys to spiritual growth is spiritual reading. When one struggles with reading comprehension, spiritual reading takes longer and is less effective than it otherwise would be.

---

101   I have, however, planned my next two meals while praying the Rosary.

102   or an explanation on fidget toys, see the chapter entitled, "Prayer Tips."

MASSive DIFFICULTIES

"[W]e should offer worship pleasing to God in reverence and awe." – Hebrews 12:28

The Rush

One of the things I enjoy doing is getting to Mass early, so I have time to kneel down and pray for a few moments to ready myself for the sacrifice of the Mass. This desire is rarely fulfilled, though. As a result of time blindness, I (and probably others like me) frequently find myself running late, resulting in me walking into the sanctuary around the same time the priest is doing so. This unnecessary stress right before what should be a pleasurable experience causes difficulties in preparing oneself for prayer. We arrive at Mass without enough time to enter into a proper state of mind, and many distractions ensue.

Memory Gaps

Distractions during Mass can cause difficulties with remembering important moments of the Mass. Sometimes ADHDers can get so lost in our thoughts that we totally space out and can have gaps in our memory. This is especially likely when it is something we have done many times (e.g. driving to school/work, walking the dog, etc.). Mass is, more or less, the same every time.[103] If we space out during Mass, we can have no recollection of certain parts of the Mass. This is especially disheartening when we have no recollection of the consecration. One area that is especially prone to being the victim of memory gaps is the homily. Most of the time, those of us with ADHD are not completely focused on the homily. We fade in and out of attention during a homily and will catch only bits and pieces of the homily.

The Case of the Disappearing Homily

Even when we do pay attention to the homily, there is a chance we will not remember a word of it. ADHD causes major problems with one's working memory. We can pay attention to a teacher's instructions on an assignment or a parent's instructions to keep the laundry moving while they go run an errand, but when it comes time to carry out those commands, we cannot remember to actually do it. There have been many times where I was focused on a priest's homily and thought it was amazing. Then, after Mass, someone will comment on what an excellent homily it was, and I will agree. Immediately after agreeing, I find myself thinking, Wait, what did Father preach

---

103   That does not mean your parish should change things up and make Mass more exciting to cater to the ADHD crowd. Keep the Mass the way the Church intends it to be. We will have distractions no matter what. Aim for reverence, not excitement. And, by the way, Jesus becoming present at the Mass is exciting (if we fully comprehend what is going on in front of us).

about again?

Noticing All the Things at Mass

As I mentioned in the chapter "What is ADHD?", it is hypothesized that, in the early days of the human race, when we were struggling to survive, it was beneficial to have what is called "floating attention." This behavior is characterized by not being completely focusing on one thing, but rather having a little bit of our attention on everything around us. Scientists use this to explain how ADHD brains work. When I attend Mass, I can see where they are coming from on this issue. The kids squirming behind me, the mother telling them to sit still, the old lady whispering the words to the Eucharistic prayer, the altar server who clearly has no clue what to do, that guy with the cough who sounds like he is dying and is not covering his mouth like any decent human being would, that cute girl I have never seen before,[104] people I know, people I do not know, the priest's new haircut, any change in the sanctuary's decorations. I. NOTICE. THEM. ALL.

Sitting in the Front Row

One thing I do that helps me focus during Mass is to sit as close to the front row as possible. Sitting in the front decreases the likelihood that I will be distracted by other people in the sanctuary.[105]When you are sitting near the back, you see everyone. You see them fidgeting. You see them leaning over to whisper something to the person next to them. And, you see them praying more devoutly than you.

However, sitting in the front means you need to sit still. Everyone is behind you. They can see you. If you are fidgeting or feel the need to get up and pace during the readings or the homily, they will see that, and you will distract them. Sitting in the back gives you the ability to stand up and pace during the readings and the homily, something that could help those with ADHD focus. However, if you are sitting in the back, you will see everything in the pews in front of you which will distract you, and you are far away from the altar, where Jesus becomes substantially present.

I have just described the positives and negatives of sitting both in the front of the sanctuary and the back of the sanctuary. In short, there is not an ideal place for ADHDers to sit during Mass. Those of you with ADHD should examine your specific needs[106] and choose your spot based on that. I do not feel the need to pace, so I choose to sit up front.

Round Parishes

My former parish is a round parish. The altar is in the middle of the sanctuary, and there are pews com-

---

104   I never seem to have the guts to talk to her, though.

105   Also, sitting in the front puts me closer to the altar, the spot where Jesus becomes substantially present. I have never understood why people, even the most devout people, prefer to sit in the back. Jesus is going to be up front! Why would you not want to be close to that?

106   Reminder: Everyone experiences ADHD differently.

pletely surrounding it. A recent renovation made it less round,[107] but you can still see people sitting across from you no matter where you sit. When you look straight ahead and see other people, it is super distracting. That is not a good thing, and it was a contributing factor to my switch to another parish.

---

107   A statement that only makes sense if you have been in this parish both before and after the renovations

EVERYDAY LIFE STRUGGLES

"We are afflicted in every way, but not constrained; perplexed, but not driven to despair; persecuted, but not abandoned; struck down, but not destroyed." – 2 Corinthians 4:8-9

More Than Just Spiritual Issues

On top of the spiritual struggles those with ADHD face, problems in our day-to-day activities also cause us distress. These everyday life struggles can bleed over and wreak havoc in our spiritual lives. It is even harder to concentrate on prayer when you are behind on multiple projects on which you are supposed to be working.

Hypersensitivity

One common problem that plagues those with ADHD is hypersensitivity. Although it is not a diagnostic criterion for ADHD, many do claim hypersensitivity to be a part of the ADHD experience, despite little to no scientific evidence to back up this claim. I discuss emotional hypersensitivity in the chapter "Emotional Struggles," but there is more to an ADHDer's hypersensitivity than just emotional sensitivity.

Those with ADHD are more prone to be hypersensitive with regards to their senses, allergies, and information. These hypersensitivities can make life difficult. Lights will be too bright. Sounds will be too loud. Certain types of clothing will be uncomfortable. Odors will be fouler. Allergic reactions will be more severe. Too much information will be overwhelming.[108]

Relationships

ADHD can also wreak havoc on relationships. Making friends can be hard for those with ADHD.[109] Thinking before we speak is not our strong suit. The impulsive blurting out of words can rub people the wrong way. Sometimes we get so wrapped up in what we are doing,[110] we forget to respond to text messages or other forms of communication.[111] We intend to respond, but we do not do so until sometimes hours later (if at all). Sometimes, boredom and/or lack of stimulation can cause ADHDers to subconsciously do things to cause drama, just to fill an instinctual need for stimulation. These struggles can also apply to familial and dating relationships.

---

108   Some people believe these struggles could be part of a separate disorder called sensory processing disorder. See the chapter entitled "Unwanted Tag-Alongs" for more information.

109   It is even harder when you are very much an introvert, like me.

110   See the "Hyperfocus" section of the chapter "What is ADHD?"

111   This may sound familiar to some readers who know me.

In the case of dating relationships, these struggles can be particularly tricky. There are higher standards in a dating relationship than in friendships, and when an ADHDer exhibits the problem behaviors listed above, it is even harder to maintain a relationship. Additionally, in the beginning of a dating relationship, an ADHDer can be intently focused on the new relationship, but after the novelty wears off, the dedication the ADHDer has wanes. The ADHDer might even break up with their significant other because of the boredom, despite the lack of problems in the relationship.

Forgetfulness

Those of us with ADHD forget things or lose items kind of a lot. Things that were in our hands two seconds ago tend to be lost all of a sudden. If we set an object down, there is no guarantee we will remember we set it there. When we put something where we do not typically place that object, it is almost guaranteed that we will struggle to find it when we need it again. Then, when it comes to looking for that object, we do not look for it in the spot where we left it. "Oh, I would never have put it there," we tell ourselves. But, we did put it there, and it will take us forever to find it[112]. This is why we need things like keyrings or bowls to hold our keys and a myriad of folders to keep various papers. Our brains to do not have the necessary number of folders to organize information in our head properly. Therefore, we need to create filing systems outside of our brain to compensate for this deficit.

Sometimes we can even forget to eat. As a writer, one of the things for which I have to be on guard is those days where I am on a roll all day.[113] Those are the danger days. If I am on a roll, I do not want to lose the hyperfocus that is helping me get stuff done. I could be hyperfocusing all day, and when I finally stop writing, I eat my first meal of the day, take my dogs outside, and go to bed.[114]

One lie those of us with ADHD tell ourselves is, "Oh, I'll do that later." The task we are supposed to do does not interest us at that time, and we decide to wait to accomplish it at a later time. Most of the time, the more convenient time does not occur before it is too late, and our decision to put off doing it comes back to haunt us. If the task in question is something important, this becomes a serious problem. This can wreak havoc on our relationships, school work, careers, finances, and spiritual lives. I know this has played an adverse role on my prayer life. When I tell myself, "I'll pray later," I know in the back of my mind that there is a good chance I will not get around to praying until just before I go to sleep, and with my propensity to stay up too late, I know it is likely I will only be able to muster up a Hail Mary and maybe a prayer to my guardian angel before I need to get in bed. A rushed prayer or two before one collapses into sleep does not make for a good spiritual life.

---

112   I recently purchased a device that I duct-taped to my TV's remote control that beeps when I press a button on a separate remote because I searched basically my entire house for an hour trying to find the dang thing, only to discover it had somehow managed to get trapped in the back part of a recliner that was closed up by Velcro.

113   Something that does not happen as often as I would like.

114   This has actually happened to me more than once. I get done writing, and I am super hungry. After eating something, my dogs and I go for a walk, and then I go to bed way later than I should.

Crime

Studies have shown a link between ADHD and crime. Estimates have placed the rate of ADHD among prison inmates around 25%.[liii] This is a much higher rate of occurrence than that for adults in the general population. ADHD has also been linked to recidivism (a fancy word for repeat offending).[liv] The impulsivity from which ADHDers suffer increases the likelihood of risky behavior, which could[115] include criminal activity.

Medication Refills

In order for me to refill my Concerta prescription, I have to call my pharmacy and request that they fax my doctor's office. Then, the pharmacy has to actually fax[116] my doctor's office.[117] Once my doctor's office gets the fax, they have to create the magic piece of paper that says I can have my medication and have a doctor sign it. There is no consistency with regards to how quickly this is accomplished. Then, they have to mail that piece of paper to my pharmacy, and we all know how the United States Postal Service is known for their speed and reliability. Oh, wait! No, they are not.[118] When/If the pharmacy receives the aforementioned magic piece of paper, they have to put 30 pills in an orange bottle which takes longer than you'd think. Then, they have to inform me that I need to take time out of my day to drive to the pharmacy and pick up my medication. Once I do that, this ridiculously long process mercifully reaches its conclusion.

At any point in the above-mentioned process, a snafu or a delay could occur, and the consequences of either of those are potentially dire. When those with ADHD are without their medication, they become less productive at work and/or school and are at a greater risk of committing a crime or engaging in other risky behaviors. Additionally, if sufferers of ADHD go unmedicated, they frequently self-medicate, meaning they turn to drugs and/or alcohol. Moreover, those with ADHD struggle with day-to-day tasks, such as remembering to get the ridiculously long process of getting a refill of their prescription going early enough so they do not run out of pills. Therefore, if all of these laws are designed to keep society safe from those who abuse ADHD medication, they probably do not help as they leave medicated ADHD sufferers without medication and cause some to give up medication entirely because of the ridiculous process of getting a refill for their prescription.[119] This leads to the aforementioned dangerous behaviors.

Medication Side Effects

I am a huge proponent of using medication to manage the symptoms of ADHD, but medication is not for

---

115   NOTE: I used the word "could" and not "will." No one is destined to commit a crime.

116   Yup, a fax. What year is this?

117   You would not believe how difficult this step is.

118   *rolls eyes* I could tell you many stories about the ineptitude of the USPS, but you would be reading this footnote for hours.

119   This is the place where I would like to tell you my brilliant solutions for this problem, but this book is not about my plans to fix governmental and regulatory ineptitude. If you ever have a conversation with me, ask me about my solutions then.

everyone. While taking a medication designed to help control unwanted symptoms, new symptoms can emerge. These wreak havoc on a person's life and can impede the progress they are making in their fight to control the symptoms of ADHD. These side effects are described in more detail in the chapter entitled, "Medication," but for now, let me say that the side effects caused by ADHD medication are just one more burden in a long list of burdens with which a person with ADHD is forced to cope.

Sleep

ADHD is not just a daytime issue; it causes problems at night, too. Many with ADHD struggle with sleep.[120] Sometimes, we are too hyperfocused on what we are doing before bed to actually get into bed and attempt to fall asleep. There is a lie we all (whether we have ADHD or not) are prone to telling ourselves: "I will finish this one last thing, and then, I'll go to bed." I do not know how many times I have done that one thing and then thought, Well, I could do this other thing, too. I often tell that to myself several times in one evening, resulting in me staying up way later than I should. Then, when I finally get into bed, there is no guarantee I will actually fall asleep in a reasonable amount of time. Those of us with ADHD (especially those with the inattentive type) are unable to shut our brains off and fall asleep. I could never fall asleep as a little kid. I would lay there for what seemed like a really long time to me, give up, and go downstairs to tell my mom that I could not sleep. I realized years later that my ADHD brain would not stop thinking.[121]

On the other hand, it might not just be our brains that refuse to shut down. Other body parts will be too active and restless to be able to calm down, lie down, and fall asleep. Those with ADHD (especially those with the hyperactive/impulsive type) can find themselves feeling an intense need to get up and move around when they are trying to fall asleep. Also, grinding one's teeth while sleeping is another common behavior that wreaks havoc on the sleep cycle of a person with ADHD.

Moreover, waking up is difficult for us, too. Even if we set an alarm, there is no guarantee we will wake up.[122] I currently have an alarm clock set to go off and my phone set to go off more than once per morning. All of these alarms go off on random intervals, and I will hit the snooze button for almost all of them.[123] My waking up process takes over thirty minutes.[124] In order to combat the difficulties of waking up, many websites that offer tips for ADHD

---

120   In fact, trouble sleeping was, at one point in time, a diagnostic criterion for ADHD

121   Have you ever thought about how amazing the human hand is? Twenty-seven bones enclosed by muscle and skin, and somehow, they can work together to do amazing things like grab a cup of water and bring it to the mouth to drink, type these words on a laptop computer, or perform open-heart surgery. Look at an X-ray of the hand and examine how those bones are connected. Some people try to say that happened by chance. To which I say, horse hockey! Those people do not understand probability. (Side note: Sir Isaac Newton once tried to calculate the odds of the world coming into existence and human beings evolving from primordial slime without a creator. Before he finished, he was baptized.) You see, this is why I could never fall asleep at night. I was too busy thinking about stuff.

122   Just ask my friend about the time he was staying at my apartment and had the pleasure of listening to my alarm going off for thirty minutes because I did not hear it.

123   What is scary about this process is that sometimes I am too tired to realize I am actually turning my alarm off and not actually hitting the snooze button. I write these words on a day where, for the second day in a row, I did just that and consequently overslept.

124   Dear future wife, we have some things to discuss regarding alarms.

management advocate using a special alarm clock that is particularly annoying and/or loud or one that slowly lights up your room as your wake-up time approaches or shakes your bed.[125]

The biggest concern with ADHD and sleep is not the sleep issues themselves; it is the effect the sleep issues have. One of the best things a person with ADHD can do to help control their ADHD symptoms (aside from taking medication) is to get a good night's sleep. First of all, you will wake up more refreshed[126] and will have fewer issues waking up and getting out of bed.[127] Additionally, when one has had a good amount of sleep the night before, any person (whether they have ADHD or not) is able to concentrate better during the day.[128] The most significant effect I have noticed a good night's sleep has had on me is the boost of effectiveness it gives my medication. If I get a good amount of sleep, my medication is much more effective.

I No Can Adult

As one ages into maturity and takes on more responsibilities, one has to do activities that the kids on the internet are grouping together and calling "adulting." As mentioned in the "What Is ADHD?" chapter, those of us with ADHD have trouble with executive functions. This makes it hard to pay bills, manage money, maintain relationships, hold down jobs, and do things most adults can do with little effort.

Choice

When you have ADHD, there are a lot of things that capture your attention, and you want to explore everything. So, when you are presented with a choice, especially a choice with many, many options, it can be hard to decide which option to choose. Everything is amazing[129] (and in other cases, everything is awful), and you want to consider each possible option. You often do not have the time to think about all of your choices as much as you would like. It can either be paralyzing, or it can lead to an impulsive decision that you will end up regretting. I was once invited to two social events that were occurring at the same time.[130] In my eyes, neither one was a better option than the other one, so I ended up staying home that night.[131] Do not even get me started on picking a restaurant when you do not have a craving for a particular food. That is pure agony.

---

125 I purchased an alarm clock that has a small disc-like object attached to it via a cord. This disc-like object vibrates when the alarm goes off. It has worked well for me when I have remembered to set that alarm before bed.

126 Allegedly

127 Again, allegedly

128 Once more, allegedly

129 Is this where we get the "Oooh, shiny!" ADHD stereotype?

130 The high school version of myself is seething with jealousy right now.

131 The high school version of myself wants to punch me in the face right now.

Impulsive Spending

I have not looked it up, but I imagine Amazon had a bit of a sales dip at the end of Quarter 1 of Fiscal Year 2017 that carried into the first few days of Quarter 2. Fiscal Year 2017 was the year I gave up online shopping[132] for Lent. I buy stuff on Amazon a lot. If a week goes by when a package from Amazon is not delivered to me, that is a victory in self-control.

The impulsive side of ADHD can wreak havoc on our wallets. My relationship with Amazon is probably similar to others' relationships with Amazon, Target, eBay, and many other places where one can easily get carried away with spending. Reigning in impulsivity when treating ADHD is especially important when impulsive shopping becomes a problem.

Crazy Conversations

While telling a story, I can go off on tangents and tell side stories.[133] This is all, of course, after giving you the setup story to the actual story. I have had many funny stories fall flat because the way I told them was confusing[134].

Those of us with ADHD can also bring up conversation topics that appear to come out of nowhere, yet we believe it was a logical train of thought. If we are talking about hot dogs and I suddenly ask you if have ever seen *The Phantom of the Opera,*[135] that seems to me like a perfectly reasonable question to ask that point in time. You might find it odd because your mind did not go down this train of thought:

Mmmm....hot dogs. Where's a good place to get hot dogs? Chicago. Chicago dogs! The Cubs play in Chicago. Didn't they once have an Australian player on their team? I've never been to Australia, but I do know that the Sydney Opera House is in Australia. I have never really thought about attending any operatic performances. I do like musical theater, though. Phantom is kind of like a cross between musical theater and opera, isn't it? Have you ever seen The Phantom of the Opera?

While you stare quizzically at me and answer my random question, I will be singing songs from *The Phantom of the Opera*[136] in my head, or out loud, probably out loud.[137]

These odd conversations confuse people. Some people are even put off by these conversations, causing difficulties when it comes to making friends and maintaining friendships. We do notice when people pull away. We may not know why a person has pulled away, but we notice when they do.

---

132   Technically, I allowed myself to shop online if I was buying a present for someone else.

133   Once, while telling a story, I stopped myself from getting into three side stories (HOORAY MEDICATION!). However, my friends were interested in hearing those side stories, and we agreed to circle back to them. I was afraid of forgetting what those side stories were, so my friends held up physical reminders to help me remember what I was going to say.

134   I told them the only way I knew how. Only a Vulcan mind meld could have relayed the story in a coherent manner.

135   +10 points if you have

136   *"Think of meeee. Think of me fooondly when we say gooooood niiiiiiiight. Remember me every so ooooften. Prooomise me yooooooou'll tryyyyy"*

137   My friends will attest that this is a common occurrence.

Time Management

If the ADHDer in your life is always late, know that they are not the only ones. Poor time management is a problem almost all ADHDers have. There are three key explanations for our lack of time management skills: Time blindness, mental paralysis, and avoidance procrastination.

ADHDers have no concept of time. We constantly misestimate the amount of time it will take us to do a task. This character trait has been dubbed "time blindness." In short, we do not have internal clocks, and if we do, they do not even come close to functioning correctly.

Mental paralysis occurs when there is so much to do that it becomes overwhelming. Having too many things to do (especially when it comes to complicated tasks that require a lot of focus) can create the situation previously discussed in this chapter under the heading "Choice" where the multitude of options or things to do makes it hard to make a choice on which task to do first. Trying to figure out what to do can cause us to do nothing, even when the choice seems clear: Go to the thing you were supposed to attend.

When a task requires a lot of effort and sustained focus, an ADHDer will probably dread doing it. They might be good at it and/or actually want to do it, but the effort needed to execute the task properly becomes overwhelming. This causes us to engage in avoidance procrastination. A friend recently described avoidance procrastination as "anything but that syndrome." Instead of doing the thing we are supposed to do, we do everything else we can think of doing. When it is time to leave for work, the thought of doing various projects or interacting with difficult co-workers might cause us to straighten the large hallway mirror we know has been crooked for months. During my academic years, studying for finals meant it was time to go bowling or clean my apartment.

You should be understanding that we are often tardy, but do not let us know you expect us to be late. Learning that you have become "the one that is always late" is demoralizing. We can find the flimsiest excuse for getting down on ourselves. We do not need your help finding reasons to feel shame. Be patient with us, and if we are open to it, help us engage in practices that will help us learn time management skills.

Busy Is Bad-ish

Having too much going on is stressful for those of us with ADHD. Remember: We have troubles keeping our emotions in check. We do not like to be overloaded. We do need structure and something to prevent boredom, but when there is too much on our plate, we become paralyzed.[138] I do not like having an unproductive day; I want to feel like I accomplished something. However, if I am always running from one thing to another, I feel overwhelmed. If I am busy from the time I wake up until the time I should go to bed, I feel off, and I feel the need to do something fun just for me. My brain needs time to unwind.[139]

---

138   ADHDers need to follow the Goldilocks rule: Not too much. Not too little. Just enough.

139   Some of this "Me-time" stuff comes from my introversion. However, ADHDers do need time for unstructured fun every day, especially if that fun comes in the form of physical exercise.

Shifting Between Tasks

Those with ADHD have trouble moving from one task to another. Whether they are hyperfocusing on a task or not, shifting one's attention from Task A to Task B is not easy. The amount of effort a non-hyperfocusing ADHDer needs to exert to stay on task is great and difficult to shift onto another task. Moreover, an ADHDer has difficulty initiating tasks. Therefore, getting started on a new task is difficult at any time, and when initiating a new task after working on something else, the difficulty only increases.

Accident-Prone

If you know someone who has ADHD, you may have noticed that they tend to be clumsy at times. This is something that affects a lot of people with ADHD. We can be accident-prone. In fact, I remembered to add something about this topic in this book only after I misjudged where the doorway to my bathroom was.[140] As I mentioned in the chapter "Unwanted Tag-Alongs," half of children who are diagnosed with ADHD are also diagnosed with a disorder that affects the development of motor skills.

---

140   I thought for sure my forehead was going to start bleeding.

PART THREE:
RISING

SUFFERING SUCKS, BUT THAT'S OKAY

"I consider that the sufferings of this present time are as nothing compared with the glory to be revealed for us."
— Romans 8:18

"If This Is How You Treat Your Friends..."

Saint Teresa of Ávila is widely regarded as one of the holiest persons to have ever lived, yet even she had her struggles with God. One day she was on a journey and fell in the mud. Depending on who is telling the story, her response to getting muddy was either a complaint to God or a conversation with God. Either way the story is told, it ends with Saint Teresa telling God that, if this is how He treats His friends, "It is no wonder why You have so few!"

We all suffer. Even the saints suffered, and some might say the saints especially suffered. It often seems like those who love God the most suffer the most. This is baffling. Shouldn't God be the kindest to those who love Him the most? We must remember what happened to the One who loved God the Father the most. He, Jesus Christ, was crucified. Christ's suffering and death was the supreme act of love, and it came via a method of execution the Romans designed to be the most painful death possible. Through Christ's passion and death, we learn a distressing truth: To love means to suffer.

Love Hurts

To love means to be vulnerable, to open yourself up to being hurt. In any romantic relationship or potential relationship, there is an ever-present risk of getting one's heart broken. Even in relationships that endure, there are heartbreaks. There are struggles. When a loved one suffers, we suffer too. Seeing them hurting hurts us. Jesus suffered, and He invites us into His suffering.

Because God loves us and we are called into a loving relationship with Him, we will suffer. "You will be hated by all because of My name," Jesus warns us in the tenth chapter of Matthew's Gospel. In short, Jesus calls us to pick up our cross and follow Him. It may not always make sense why Jesus makes those closest to Him suffer, but we can find hints as to why this happens.

Humility

Saul thought he was doing the Lord's work. He believed he was ridding the world of a heresy that was separating people from God, but then the Lord knocked Saul off of his high horse, both literally and figuratively. When Saint Paul fell off his horse on the road to Damascus, he lost the ability to see. He was humbled. Someone needed to lead him, to guide him. When he eventually regained his sight, he also gained a new world view. In being humbled in this way, Paul realized he did not know everything. He learned that the very thing he was persecuting was the very thing the world needed.

We can be like Paul. There are times where we feel like we have everything figured out. We know what's what. Then, a suffering comes along and shows us the error of our thinking. Suffering humbles us. We learn because of suffering. It sure would be nice if we could learn our lesson without suffering, but would we actually ever learn our lesson if we do not experience the suffering that teaches us the lesson? I know there are some lessons I have learned in my life that I would never have learned if it was not for a suffering I endured.

Balance

Have you ever dedicated yourself to something that made you feel good? Perhaps, it was athletics. Sports can provide a healthy lifestyle, a community, and a sense of accomplishment.[141] You can feel like you are following God's will in playing that sport. He has given you a great gift, and it is providing you with many blessings. Yet, what happens if an injury occurs that ends your ability to participate in that sport? Does life go on? Are you able to find healthy ways of spending your time if you are unable to participate in your favorite sport? Or, was your identity too wrapped up in the sport you played? God can take away beautiful parts of your life to remind you that our happiness and identity are found only in Him. When we suffer, we are called to examine our lives. Do our wills align with God's will? Have we neglected our relationship with God in favor of another relationship or a hobby? Where are our priorities? A period of suffering can be an excellent opportunity to examine some of these questions and see if there is a lack of balance in your life.

Patience

As the philosopher Mick Jagger once said, "You can't always get what you want."[142] When we suffer, we desire for our suffering to end immediately, yet we are rarely in control of when our suffering will end. The desire to see the pain cease goes unfulfilled, and we are stuck waiting. In these moments, we need to be patient. However, it is rare for us[143] to have the necessary patience to wait for our sufferings to end. This forces us to wait, and the natural result of an impatient person being forced to wait is growth in patience. I have often wondered just how one can grow in patience, and I am starting to come to the inconvenient realization that one grows in patience when one is forced to be patient.

---

141   That is assuming one is good at the sport in question

142   I should point out here that, in the first episode of *House, M.D.*, the title character makes this same point, and I would not have thought to say that unless I had watched that episode. Senator Angus King (I-Maine) also quoted Jagger on the Senate floor during a 2013 debate over the budget, but I did not know that until I googled who first quoted the "philosopher Mick Jagger."

143   Well, I say "us," but let's be real here. I really mean me.

Strength/Beautiful Fruit

While writing this chapter, I spoke with a friend who suffers from chronic health problems. She reminded me that God allows suffering in our lives to strengthen us for something He has planned for us. As noted in the scripture verse I shared at the beginning of this chapter, our sufferings are nothing compared to the glory that God will later reveal to us. After we suffer, and in some cases, because we suffer, God can produce beautiful fruit. The key is to look for the ways God has produced beautiful things in our lives through our suffering. If we are not watching for how God is at work in our lives, we will never accept that He does work in our lives. For example, after years of suffering emotional turmoil because of my parents' divorce, I realized that my own attitudes towards marriage have been shaped by my experiences. I take the Sacrament of Matrimony more seriously than I probably would have if my parents had not divorced. The indissolubility of marriage is more firmly established in my mind. When/if I get married, I know what I will be getting myself into. Yes, it sucks having divorced parents, but my sufferings related to that are a reminder of the importance of marriage. I hope my sufferings in this area will make me a better husband someday.

Yet, if I had not taken the time to reflect on my experiences, I would never have realized that God worked for my benefit through my sufferings. Through examining our sufferings and how we are affected by them, we can more clearly see how God is at work. When we examine just the awful parts of life, it is impossible to see how an all-good God can allow such atrocities. We only see a small sliver of God's grand design. However, if we zoom out and see how good can come from bad situations, we see a more complete picture of God's plan.[144] This can sometimes lead us to be grateful for our sufferings. In fact, during the Easter Vigil, the Church makes some bold claims during The Exsultet:

> O truly necessary sin of Adam,
>
> destroyed completely by the Death of Christ!
>
> O happy fault
>
> that earned so great, so glorious a Redeemer!

Yes, you read that correctly. The Church calls the sin of Adam "necessary." We needed Original Sin to receive Jesus. Therefore, in today's world, we need to suffer so that we might be graced with the gift of Jesus Christ.

Jesus Knows Your Suffering

In his apostolic letter, Salvifici Doloris, Saint John Paul II notes that, when Jesus came to conduct His earthly mission, He intentionally drew close to those who were suffering:

His actions concerned primarily those who were suffering and seeking help. He healed the sick, consoled the afflicted, fed the hungry, freed people from deafness, from blindness, from leprosy, from the Devil and from various

---

144   Bishop Robert Barron has a good YouTube video about this.

physical disabilities, three times He restored the dead to life. He was sensitive to every human suffering, whether of the body or of the soul.

This is an important reminder that Jesus came for the suffering. He wants to assist us in our trials. The love of Christ manifests as a source of consolation for those who suffer.

Moreover, Jesus became fully human. He experienced a lot of the same sufferings we endure today.[145] He grieved at the loss of a friend, was betrayed by a friend, abandoned by His closest friends in a time of great trial, unjustly accused of a crime, and brutally executed. Jesus suffered all sorts of physical and emotional pains. In short, if you can suffer it, Jesus suffered it too. Jesus did not have ADHD, but He did suffer mental anguish. He was frustrated at times, and He was often misunderstood by those closest to Him.

Not only did Christ suffer, but He also accepted His sufferings. His prayer in the Garden of Gethsemane ended with, "Thy will be done." Jesus asked to be delivered from His passion and death but recognized that His Father's will was more important than avoiding pain. Likewise, we, too, should echo that same sentiment. Every time we pray the Our Father, we have an opportunity to imitate Christ. It can be easy to say this prayer without contemplating or comprehending exactly what we are saying when we say, "Thy Kingdom come. Thy will be done." If we fully comprehended what that means, we would either accept our sufferings or refrain from praying the Our Father.

Redemptive Suffering

One of the most beautiful things about the Catholic Church is her teaching on redemptive suffering. By uniting our sufferings to the Cross of Christ, we are sanctified. Our suffering can, therefore, bring about good for ourselves or for others. Without redemptive suffering, pain and suffering are meaningless. I could not accept the difficult things I have had to endure throughout my life without the idea of redemptive suffering.

Saint Paul, in his epistle to the Colossians (1:24-29), speaks to the truth of redemptive suffering. "Now I rejoice in my sufferings for your sake, and in my flesh I am filling up what is lacking in the afflictions of Christ on behalf of His Body, which is the Church." Joy is Paul's view of suffering. He rejoices that he is able to suffer because he knows he can unite his sufferings to those of Christ. In doing so, he recognizes he can achieve good in the lives of others. In short, his suffering takes on meaning when he offers them up and unites them to the Cross of Christ.

Offer It Up!

While growing up, I often heard the phrase, "offer it up," when something did not go the way I wanted or if I had a minor bump or bruise. This is an expression I heard both at home and in the Catholic school I attended. Yet, every time I heard it, I would wonder what it meant, why I should do it, and how one does that. No one ever explained it to me as a child.[146]

---

145   This tells us that to suffer is to be human.

146   Well, I suppose maybe someone did once, but if they did, I assume they were wrong, they gave an unsatisfying and/or unclear answer, or it went over my head.

The theology behind this expression is a bit complex for a wee youngster to understand. Now that I am older and understand it a little bit, I realize the power of this brief piece of advice. Unfortunately, the phrase "offer it up" has become almost trite in the Church today and is, therefore, often dismissed or the inspiration for a chuckle. What we have forgotten is the awe-inspiring invitation that is the exhortation to "offer it up." To "offer it up" is to unite your suffering with those of Christ on the Cross. When we suffer, Jesus invites us into the redemptive act. God is glorified when His creatures cooperate with His divine plan.

In offering it up, you should have a specific intention. It can be simply to ask for strength to get through your trial or another intention for yourself. In an act of great love, you can offer up your sufferings for others. For example, if someone is unjustly attacking you, you can offer up your suffering for them so that they might come to know the error of their ways and be drawn into the Lord's loving embrace.[147] Moreover, if you are suffering in one aspect of life, you could offer up your sufferings for someone you know who is suffering a more severe pain in another aspect of life. For example, if you break a pinky toe, you could offer your pain for someone with cancer.

Knowing you can offer up your sufferings can give you the strength to endure your sufferings and even turn the tables on your suffering. When you offer up your sufferings, you are putting yourself in a position of power with respect to how you will respond to your pain. Instead of just letting your suffering attack you, you are now on the offensive. You are now putting yourself (and others if you offer up your sufferings for them) in a position to receive graces from the Lord. Moreover, offering up your suffering gives you the courage to endure whatever crap is being thrown your way. In a certain sense, you adopt a bring-it-on attitude or a Satan-ain't-got-nothin'-on-me attitude. In short, offering up your suffering and uniting them to the Cross of Christ strengthens you.

Remedy for Suffering = Jesus

When suffering arises, it is common for us to ask, "Why?" Often, it seems that God provides no answer to this question. Every author I have read with something valid to say on the subject of suffering says that all the signs point to Jesus as being the answer to suffering.[148] In Him, our suffering finds meaning and can be redeemed. It is in Christ that Saint Paul found joy in his sufferings.[149]

Jesus knows our suffering, and we can make our suffering redemptive by uniting our sufferings to His. Therefore, the remedy and sure means of peace in our trials is embracing Christ. Our Lord Jesus Christ came to suffer and die for us that we might have hope, rise above suffering, and have eternal life with Him. Saint John Paul II, in the aforementioned apostolic exhortation, says:

As a result of Christ's salvific work, man exists on earth with the hope of eternal life and holiness. And even though the victory over sin and death achieved by Christ in His Cross and Resurrection does not abolish temporal suffering

---

147   Have I ever offered my sufferings for someone who was persecuting me? This hypocrite declines to comment.

148   Yep, that old Sunday School trick of putting Jesus down for every answer actually has a real-life application.

149   I would give you a quote here, but there are so many throughout his writings. I feel I would be leaving out the most appropriate one if I gave you several examples but not all of them. If I gave you all of these quotes, it would be a far too long list.

from human life, nor free from suffering the whole historical dimension of human existence, it nevertheless throws a new light upon this dimension and upon every suffering: the light of salvation…God the Father has loved the only-begotten Son, that is, He loves Him in a lasting way; and then in time, precisely through this all-surpassing love, He "gives" this Son, that He may strike at the very roots of human evil and thus draw close in a salvific way to the whole world of suffering in which man shares.

Christ suffered for us, to draw us to Himself. Think of suffering as a call to union with Jesus. He is the key to enduring our struggles. Uniting our sufferings to the Cross of Christ will bring us peace. Through coming to Him in our weakness, Christ lifts us up and gives us new life through our weaknesses.

Jesus stretched out His arms on the Cross, and that act of stretching out His hands can be thought of as Him opening His arms to embrace us.[150] In His loving embrace, we can find all that we need to survive and thrive despite our sufferings. When it seems like the world is crashing down on you, remember the words of Christ: "[T]ake courage, I have conquered the world."[lv]

Comforter of the Afflicted

If you are suffering or someone you know is suffering, I would also suggest turning to the Comforter of the Afflicted, Mary. Turning to our Blessed Mother and seeking her intercession in times of sorrow can be of great benefit. She knows suffering. She watched her Son suffer the most horrendous death imaginable. In short, Mary knows your pain, for she, too, has suffered. On the Cross, Christ gave her to us as a mother. Accept her motherly love. She wants to comfort you in your afflictions. Let her.

In Suffering, There Is Hope

The important thing to remember with ADHD or any disorder/illness/disease/disability is that God allows these sufferings to open up pathways for grace to enter into our lives. According to the DSM-V, 5% of children and 2.5% of adults have ADHD.[151] This means that, if you have ADHD, you are in a small minority. God has given you something few people have. Therefore, the graces you will receive by embracing this cross will be much different from the vast majority of other people who receive graces from embracing more common crosses. These graces allow us to do amazing things for the kingdom of God that hardly anyone else gets to do. How will you use the gifts God has given you?

In the midst of suffering or simply when you feel stuck, it is beneficial to remember that your trials are not purposeless. God is at work, and He is working for your benefit. When you are suffering, keep an eye out for how the

---

150   Yes, I know that sounds cheesy. Part of me died while typing that out. But, the metaphor works, so I went for it. Don't @ me.

151   One would think that the percentage of children and the percentage of adults who have ADHD would be close to identical because few individuals grow out of ADHD. I wish I had a scientific answer for that conundrum, but I do not. However, I will say that ADHD is highly undiagnosed in adults. Therefore, as time goes on and more children become adults, those numbers will grow closer to each other. Furthermore, ADHD is highly heritable. It could be that the prevalence of ADHD is increasing due to like-minded individuals (or, rather, similarly wired brains) meeting, falling in love, and reproducing. That is my unscientific opinion on the matter.

Lord is at work. If you do, you will see Him working, and it will be totally freaking awesome.

WHY ME?

"Consider it all joy, my brothers, when you encounter various trials, for you know that the testing of your faith produces perseverance. And let perseverance be perfect, so that you may be perfect and complete, lacking in nothing. But if any of you lacks wisdom, he should ask God who gives to all generously and ungrudgingly, and he will be given it. But he should ask in faith, not doubting, for the one who doubts is like a wave of the sea that is driven and tossed about by the wind."
– James 1:2-6

Questioning God

When we realize we have ADHD, it can be tempting to cry, "WHY ME?!" It is not a bad question to ask. Too often, it seems like we are commanded to follow God's will without an explanation. There is no reason why we cannot ask God why he has given the cross we are to bear. Yes, we are to carry out God's will no matter what, but there is no reason we cannot ask for an explanation. In fact, I think it is easier to follow His commands when you know why He has given them to you. He may not give you an answer, but as long as you are genuinely listening for an answer,[152] it does not hurt to ask.

Why Me? As in. Why Alex?

"Have you ever asked Me why you have ADHD?" God asked me one day while I was on a retreat.

"No," I replied.

"Might be a good idea to do that," God said.[153]

When I brought the "Why me?" question to God in prayer, I found that ADHD humbled me. I realized that, if I did not have ADHD, I would not feel a need for God.[154] I would be left trying to do everything myself. By giving me ADHD as a challenge,[155] God showed me that I cannot do everything and reminded me that I need His help. When I underwent tests for ADHD, one of the things they did was measure my IQ to get an understanding of how I should be performing in the areas that are hampered by ADHD, and I scored in the 98th percentile.[156] I was also told people with a high IQ are prone to arrogance and feelings of independence and superiority. Therefore, the fact that God allowed ADHD in my life is indicative of a plan to humble me and prevent a majority of those types

---

152   I know I cannot be the only one who has ever angrily asked God, "Why is this happening?" and then never actually listened for a response. Your heart has to be truly open to hearing His will. If you do not accept the possibility that God is working for your best interests in whatever crisis you are enduring, no explanation will ever satisfy you.

153   Okay, that is not exactly how it went down. God and I do not have back-and-forths like that. It is usually Him sitting there waiting for me to realize what He has been trying to tell me for a while now and then laughing at me (I feel like He does that a lot with me) when I finally say, "Why didn't I realize that sooner?!"

154   I would still need God—everyone does—but I would be too arrogant to realize it.

155   It is, indeed, a challenge. See the chapter entitled, "A Cross, Not a Superpower."

156   A result that surprised me

of feelings.[157]

Furthermore, I need a challenge. Through prayer, I have learned that, if I am honest with myself, I do not want God to make things easy for me. God gave me this inquisitive mind of mine, and if I do not get to use it, I sputter. My struggles in algebra classes were not due to not understanding algebra. On the contrary, I never faced a question on an algebra test that I did not know how to do. The reason I chronically underperformed in algebra was my overconfidence and carelessness in the face of easy questions. I would go too quickly and/or do the problem on autopilot, causing me to make silly mistakes. The lack of a challenge hurt my chances of succeeding. In AP Calculus, on the other hand, I performed better because that class provided me with an adequate[158] challenge.[159] It is when my mind is met with the right challenge that I am able to succeed. Having ADHD has created a scenario where my spiritual life is a challenge. I would be bored if I did not struggle to pray.

Moreover, part of my "why" might be so that I can help others. As I write these words, my friend is sitting in a doctor's office, waiting to hear if he has ADHD. I have been able to talk him through the diagnosis process and listen to his anxieties about the whole process. While reflecting on this in prayer earlier this morning, I imagined myself sitting in a doctor's office someday with my future son and explaining to him what the doctor had just told me when he was not in the room. During my one-on-one with the doctor, I asked to be the one to tell him that he has ADHD. I explained to this hypothetical child of mine that he has a "racecar brain," as Doctor Hallowell would say. I told him that it was a good brain, a powerful brain. I also told him he will struggle to control his brain and that that is okay because his dad also has a racecar brain. If God ever gives me any children with ADHD, I know I will be able to be there for them to help them through the unique scenarios those of us with ADHD face. This experience in prayer made me wonder, *Who else can I help?* Perhaps, dear reader, it is you whom I most need to help.[160] [161]Additionally, the above experiences and the process of writing this book has led me to finally find my career path. I started this book project as a freelance writer, hoping to find a more lucrative career, and now, I am an ADHD coach and own my own business, Reset ADHD.[162]

Your "Why" Will Be Different

The reason you have ADHD (or the reason your loved one has ADHD) will be different than mine. Everyone experiences ADHD differently, and I am sure God has given the gift of the cross of ADHD to each ADHDer for unique reasons. I offer my story as an example of what exploring the reasons why God is doing what He is doing

---

157   I have a friend who would be quick to point out that I do, indeed, still get arrogant from time to time.

158   Well, most of the time, the challenge was adequate. AP Calculus got a little too challenging at times.

159   I still underperformed in AP Calculus, but this time, it was the result of my propensity for spacing out during tests and not having enough time to finish.

160   Thank you for picking up this book. We can get through this together. You are not alone.

161   I hope this book has helped. If it has helped but not enough, feel free to contact me through my website, ResetADHD.com.

162   Visit ResetADHD.com to hit the reset button on your ADHD!

in one's life looks like. In examining my story, I hope you become inspired to explore this question with regards to your situation. Journeys of self-exploration and self-discovery are often difficult, but the rewards are worth the pain. A better understanding of how God is working in your life helps you embrace your cross more willingly. The weight of your cross becomes lighter, and it becomes easier[163] to trust God.

---

163   Note: I said easier and not easy. Crosses are not meant to be easy.

CREATED IN GOD'S IMAGE

"God created mankind in His image; in the image of God He created them." – Genesis 1:27

Does God Have ADHD?

The Bible tells us that we were created in the image and likeness of God. As a little kid, this is exciting because you are created like God, a being who has unlimited power. However, as you get older, you start to lose the innocence of childhood, and the meaning behind being created in the image and likeness of God becomes less clear. It is an even more difficult concept to understand when you ADHD.

Those of us who discover we have ADHD can be left wondering how we fit into the idea of being created in the image and likeness of God. If we have ADHD and are created in the image and likeness of God, what does that say about God? Does God have ADHD? If it says nothing about God, what does it say about us? If we're not perfect, are we really created in the image and likeness of God? There are no easy answers to how one is created in the image and likeness of God, especially when one struggles with ADHD. The key to overcoming any feelings of shame and doubt with regards to looking at ourselves as people with ADHD is to recognize our true identity as children of God.

Our True Identity

We do not find our identity in ADHD or any other disability, nor in our height, weight, hair color, eye color, skin color, or sexual orientation. Our true identity comes from the one who created us. Being created in the image and likeness of God gives the human person a special dignity. As the Catechism puts it:

Being in the image of God the human individual possesses the dignity of a person, who is not just something, but someone…And he is called by grace to a covenant with his Creator, to offer Him a response of faith and love that no other creature can give in his stead.

By creating us in His image, God gave us a special dignity that no other aspect of creation received. One of my favorite saints, Saint Eugène de Mazenod,[164] offered one of my favorite explanations of what it means to be created in the image and likeness of God and the dignity that flows from that:[165]

Come, then, and learn what you are in the eyes of God. All you poor of Jesus Christ, you afflicted,

---

164   Saint Eugène de Mazenod is an absolute baller! More on him later.

165   Saint Eugène said this during the first sermon of his 1814 Lenten lecture series. He wanted to offer instruction to the poor in his hometown of Aix-en-Provence, whom he felt had been neglected in the Church. "[T]he Gospel must be taught to all and it must be taught in such a way as to be understood," he said at the beginning of this sermon.

unfortunate, suffering, infirm, diseased, all you who are burdened with misery, my brothers, my very dear brothers, my respected brothers, listen to me! You are the children of God, the brothers of Jesus Christ, co-heirs of His eternal kingdom, the cherished portion of His inheritance. In the words of Saint Peter, you are the holy people, you are kings, you are priests, in a certain sense, you are gods!...For once, let your eyes look through the tatters which cover you. There is an immortal soul within you, made to the image of God Whom it is destined to possess one day; a soul redeemed at the price of the Blood of Jesus Christ, more precious in the eyes of God than all the riches of the earth, than all the kingdoms of the world; a soul He considers more desirable than the government of the entire universe.

In short, Saint Eugène tells us that to be created in the image and likeness of God—that is, to be God's children—means that we have a royal dignity that cannot be extinguished by any person or thing. We cannot define ourselves by the tragedies, disappointments, or failings of our lives. We are the children of a king, and that is where we find who we truly are.

MEDICATION

"Moses prayed for the people, and the LORD said to Moses: Make a seraph and mount it on a pole, and everyone who has been bitten will look at it and recover. Accordingly Moses made a bronze serpent and mounted it on a pole, and whenever the serpent bit someone, the person looked at the bronze serpent and recovered." – Numbers 21:7-9

Just a Reminder: I Am an ADHD Coach, Not a Doctor! [166]

I am not a doctor. Any sort of medical advice given in this chapter is just my opinion and should be taken with a grain of salt. Always consult with your doctor before beginning or ceasing a medication.

No Medication Haters Allowed!

Of all the treatment options for ADHD, the only one that has been scientifically proven for reducing and controlling the symptoms of ADHD is medication. Anyone who says they can cure you, your child, or a loved one of ADHD without using medication has something to sell you and has not adequately researched ADHD. Yes, there are non-medication options for managing the symptoms of ADHD that can help prevent an ADHDer's life from spiraling out of control, but the only treatment option that has been proven to reduce the severity of symptoms is medication. To deny a person with ADHD the option of medication is to refuse the best defense a person against the nasty symptoms of ADHD.

Judge Not, Lest Ye Be Judged

Do not judge parents who medicate their children. Those parents already face judgment for the behavior of their children when they are not medicated. It is a no-win scenario for them. You could make their lives a lot easier if you let them make a smart decision with regards to their child's healthcare.[167]

Risk of Self-Medication

If a person does not treat their ADHD, they are prone to self-medicate. The effects of undiagnosed ADHD on a person can be devastating.[168] A lifetime of being told to work harder, that they will never amount to anything, and that they are lazy takes a toll on a person. The constant state of underachievement with no hope of overcoming what they think is an attitude problem they cannot overcome creates a feeling of worthlessness. In their state of

---

166   +10 points if you caught the reference

167   *steps off soapbox*

168   See chapter "Get a Diagnosis!"

frustration and disappointment in themselves, they turn to alcohol, marijuana, and potentially other drugs to escape these lousy feelings. In fact, lack of treatment is the main reason those with ADHD abuse drugs. Those who are being treated for ADHD abuse drugs at a far lower rate than those with ADHD who are not being treated.[169]

Experimentation

Unfortunately, because not everyone experiences ADHD in the same way, it is impossible to know which medication and what dosage will be the best option for each individual patient. The doctors who treat ADHD will have the unpleasant task of experimenting to find the right type of medication and the right dosage.

The two main medications[170] for treating ADHD are amphetamine (Brand name: Adderall) and methylphenidate (Common brand names: Ritalin and Concerta). Doctors have no guidance as to which medication and which dosage should work best, and they are, therefore, forced to pick one of the two drugs, start with a low dose, and slowly increase the dosage, watching the patient carefully to make sure the medication is not causing adverse side effects. The process is neither easy nor fun.

Benefits of Medication

As mentioned above, medication is the single best remedy for ADHD symptoms. I have found this to be true. No behavioral strategy or dietary supplement has produced better results in my fight[171] to manage ADHD than medication. The first day I took medication, I noticed I was still distracted, but it was easier for me to recognize I was distracted and return to that on which I needed to focus. That was a low dosage of a different medication than the one I currently take. With a higher dosage and taking a medication I find more effective, the results are even more potent.

What Medication Cannot Do

As much as I want it to do so, medication cannot entirely remove the symptoms of ADHD. It is not a cure; it is an attempt to level the playing field between ADHDers and neurotypicals. To expect a cure is unreasonable.

Even though medication helps level the playing field, it is still difficult to reach a point where the playing field does indeed become level. As mentioned above, finding the right medication and dosage is difficult. Moreover, a person with ADHD does not know what normal is and cannot know if they are achieving results that allow them to be on the same level as neurotypicals. Furthermore, one may have to reduce the dosage of medication due to side effects. A higher dosage might be more beneficial to the individual and allow them to perform at the same level as their peers, but the severity of the side effects might make taking the most efficacious dosage impossible.

---

169   This makes the large number of regulations regarding ADHD medication seem a bit unnecessary, but I say more on that in the chapter entitled, "Everyday Life Struggles."

170   There are other medications one can take, but these two medications are usually the first two to be tried.

171   And, it is most definitely a fight. At times, one might even call it a brawl.

Medication Holidays

Some health professionals and bloggers (both qualified and unqualified to be discussing ADHD) advocate medication holidays, which are breaks from medication during parts of one's life where one is not at school or work. In these instances, a person with ADHD does not take their medication over the weekend or during summer break.

However, Doctor William Dodson, a leading expert in ADHD medications, warns against this practice. When one is away from school or work, temptations and opportunities to misbehave increase. Schools help keep kids in line. It is the behavior outside of the classroom that has the potential to get them in serious trouble. When a person is at school or work, there are fewer ways of breaking the law or engaging in dangerous behavior than outside of a structured environment. It is when ADHDers are away from structure that they most need help in controlling their impulsive side. Medication, therefore, is more important with regards to an ADHDer's safety outside of school and/ or working hours than during the school/work day. Moreover, if the ADHDer is Catholic or a practitioner of any religion that involves praying, medication will be needed to focus on that. Prayer does not typically take place during the school/work day unless the ADHDer attends a Catholic (or other private school where prayer takes place) or works for a religious institution.

Additionally, if there is a need for the child to take a medication holiday, then there is a strong possibility that the child is on the wrong medication. If there are unwanted side effects to the medication the child is currently taking, try switching medications. There are several medications one can take for ADHD. When unwanted side effects occur, it is imperative to try a different medication.

The only justification for taking a medication holiday that might have some legitimacy is taking one might help prevent tolerance. Sometimes, once a person with ADHD has taken a medication for a long time, their body becomes used to it, and the effectiveness begins to wane. Some people claim that taking medication holidays might prevent this from happening. Even if it does prevent this, the ADHDer is still prone to all of the problems I mentioned above while on a medication holiday. Therefore, it best to do a cost-benefit analysis when considering whether or not to try a medication holiday.

Medication Is Not For Everyone

With medication, comes the possibility of side effects. It is important to note that it comes with only the possibility of side effects, not the guarantee of side effects. Yes, some people do experience side effects from medication. Most people do not experience side effects or experience only minor side effects that they can comfortably tolerate. If you are worried about the side effects of taking medication, remember that the side effects of ADHD medication are not permanent. They will go away if the patient stops taking the medication.[172]

Just as we should not judge anyone who takes medication to treat ADHD, so too should we not judge anyone who ceases taking ADHD medication. I am a big proponent of taking medication to manage the symptoms of

---

172   As with all ADHD treatment options, it is best to consult with your doctor if you suspect it is time to eliminate your medication.

ADHD, but I recognize that it does not work for everyone and that there are people who cease taking it for legitimate reasons. Despite my opinion of medication, I should not and do not look down on anyone who ceases taking medication. I believe everyone[173] should at least try medication, but if it does not work[174] or causes intolerable side effects, I support the cessation of medicating and do not judge those who take that step.

Appetite

Some people lose weight while taking medication. The medications used to treat ADHD have been known to cause a loss of appetite.[175] Not everyone will experience an extreme loss of appetite. Again, everyone has a different metabolism, and medication may or may not dramatic change to one's appetite. There is no way to know. A small amount of appetite loss is not a terrible thing, especially if you have extra weight to lose. If you lose an unhealthy amount of weight, then it might be time to cease medication or try a different medication. As always, consult a doctor before making any changes on your own.

Brrrrrrnnnngh! ADHD Braaaaains!

A common complaint about ADHD medication is that it turns the person taking the medication into a zombie. The person taking the medication can lose their personality and seem like they just merely exist. This personality change causes some fear in the people using the medication and in their loved ones.[176] For some people, this is true. Those people should stop taking the medication they are taking. However, most people do not become zombies.[177]

Sleep Struggles?

One concern people have with regards to using medication to treat ADHD is the risk that the medication might make it harder for the ADHDer to fall asleep. Yes, this is a possibility. However, the ADHD brain struggles to shut down when it is time to go to sleep, so whether or not the person is taking medication, it will be difficult to fall asleep. In fact, the medication might make it easier to fall asleep. If the medication allows the brain to calm down and cease racing thoughts, it will be easier to fall asleep.

---

173   Everyone with ADHD, that is

174   There is a small percentage of the ADHD population for whom medication does not work.

175   While taking Adderall, I decided to start eating healthier. Five months after starting to eat healthier foods (and not changing my exercise habits), I had gone from weighing 177.2 pounds to 150 pounds, causing my mother to be concerned. I now take Concerta and have become less strict about what I eat, which has caused me to gain most of that weight back. It was not until I switched from Adderall to Concerta that I realized Adderall was to credit for a good amount of that weight loss. After being on Concerta for just a few days, I felt hungry all the time. Note: I did not switch medications because of the weight loss; I switched because Concerta worked better for me.

176   I have a friend with whom I did theater in high school who stopped taking his ADHD medication because he felt he performed better when he was not taking it. I did not notice a difference in my theatrical performances after I started taking medication, though.

177   PSA: A medicated zombie apocalypse should not be feared.

Euphoria

One side effect that can occur is a feeling of euphoria, an intense and exaggerated feeling of happiness, joy, pleasure, and well-being. Often the state of euphoria does not match the reality of the situation. A person may be justified in being happy, but a euphoric person is happy beyond what is appropriate for the situation. For example, the first time I took a dose of ADHD medication and actually felt it kick in, the mere fact I felt it take effect made me so happy that I spent the entire day celebrating and did not do anything productive the entire day. Another time, following a good night's sleep, I felt my medication was working so well that I felt I could have punched a mountain and the mountain would have fallen over.[178] These examples are minor examples of euphoria. For some, the feelings of euphoria are dangerous and lead to risky behavior.[179] That level of euphoria is a good indication it is time to lower the dosage of the medication, or it is time to eliminate the medication altogether.

---

178   Luckily, there are no mountains in Sioux Falls, South Dakota. Otherwise, I might have broken my hand.

179   Like, punching a mountain, for example

MEDITATION AND MINDFULNESS: MODERN MUMBO JUMBO?

"Do not conform yourselves to this age but be transformed by the renewal of your mind, that you may discern what is the will of God, what is good and pleasing and perfect." – Romans 12:2

Beware of Eastern Spirituality!

Modern psychiatric care has begun to emphasize practices such as meditation and mindfulness as part of a treatment plan for managing the symptoms of ADHD and other psychiatric conditions. This has raised some alarm because, as Catholics, we are to avoid practices that separate us from God. A lot of these practices are being taken from Eastern religions, which have a long history of clashing with Catholic spirituality.

Many concerns have been raised about some of the techniques those in the mental health field are teaching their Catholic patients. These concerns are understandable. We must be on guard because spiritual practices that are not of God can be and probably are affected by Satan.[180] If a practice opens a person up to the spiritual realm via a non-Christian method, one is in danger of spiritual ills.

Meditation

Before one can make any statements on meditation, one must clarify what is meant by meditation. This practice can have several meanings depending on how one uses it. A simple definition is to relax and focus one's mind[181] for a period of time.

Catholics do practice meditation. It is not taught well,[182] but it is an acceptable practice. We are called to meditate on the mysteries of our faith, the mysteries of the Rosary, and Scripture. However, one must be wary of what is acceptable meditation is and what methods of meditation are not in line with Catholic spirituality. Many of the meditation practices that have become popular over the past fifty years or so have their roots in eastern spiritual-ity, which is fraught with spiritual dangers. One of the most popular ones that we Catholics should avoid is sitting in poses and chanting phrases (or the names of Hindu deities) that have roots in Buddhist and Hindu spirituality. This practice, which seeks to empty the mind, opens a person up to spiritual attacks. Catholic meditation seeks to fill one's mind with thoughts of God and His love for us.

---

180   This is not a scare tactic. The influence of the devil is real and affects the world in ways we do not always recognize. An excellent book to learn more about this is *An Exorcist Explains the Demonic: The Antics of Satan and His Army of Fallen Angels* by Father Gabriele Amorth. WARNING: This book is not an easy ready. Satan will try to get you to stop reading it.

181   Relaxing and focusing one's mind can be difficult for an ADHD mind, but the more you practice this, the more you are able to slow down and meditate and know what meditation techniques work for you. Not all meditation techniques are the same. Some people meditate while moving.

182   Or, like, at all

Mindfulness

Mindfulness is another term that does not have a clear definition. If you do a Google search for the definition of mindfulness, you will find many explanations for the concept of mindfulness. All of the definitions have the common theme of becoming more aware of the present moment.

The question of "Can Catholics practice mindfulness?" is a topic that is much discussed on the internet. There does not appear to be a clear consensus, and there are no official Church teachings on it. Those who are against its use claim it has Buddhist roots. Dan Burke, president of the Avila Institute for Spiritual Formation, says that, while there is nothing wrong with mindfulness per se, it does not offer the fullness of faith that Catholic spirituality offers. There are those, though, that point to some eastern philosophies and religions that practice mindfulness and declare that, because the practice of mindfulness is a part of eastern religions, Catholics should not engage in this practice.

Doctor Gregory Bottaro, founder of the Catholic Psych Institute and author of *The Mindful Catholic: Finding God One Moment at a Time*,[183] teaches a class on Catholic mindfulness. He defines mindfulness as "paying attention to the present moment without judgment or criticism." His book teaches Catholics to be aware of the present moment, specifically what is going on inside and outside of themselves. By reading his books, Catholics are taught to pay attention to how they are feeling physically and emotionally, what they are thinking, how they are being distracted, and how God is working in their life.

A 2017 book, A Catholic Guide to Mindfulness by Susan Brinkmann, presents a contrary opinion to that of Doctor Bottaro. She argues that Catholics absolutely should not practice mindfulness. However, her explanation of what mindfulness is reveals her lack of proper research into the topic. Moreover, her arguments against mindfulness are circular. The general gist of her argument against mindfulness runs something like this: Catholics should practice Catholicism. Catholics should not practice mindfulness because it is not a Catholic practice. Mindfulness was started by a Buddhist based on his religious beliefs. Mindfulness has Buddhist roots. Buddhism is not Catholicism. Therefore, Catholics should not practice mindfulness.

What is striking to me is how much Battaro and Brinkmann agree. They both justify their positions by stating that mindfulness is not prayer and by pointing to Vatican II's the Declaration on the Relation of the Church with Non-Christian Religions of the Second Vatican Council, Nostra Aetate. Also, they both hold up Brother Lawrence's *The Practice of the Presence of God: The Best Rule of Holy Life*[184] as an example of proper spirituality. Battaro states it is a Catholic version of mindfulness, and Brinkmann claims it is a Catholic alternative to mindfulness.

My Thoughts

With psychology's big push on meditation and mindfulness, it can be hard to know what to do as a Catholic.

---

183   Doctor Peter Kreeft wrote the forward for this book. If he wrote a forward for a book on mindfulness for Catholics, then I am willing to say mindfulness, at least as Doctor Bottaro describes it, is not only acceptable but also worth exploring.

184   Incidentally, it is a book I highly recommend.

One essential thing is communication with your doctor, therapist, and/or coach. If you are worried about heading down a dangerous path, explain to them that your Catholic faith does not allow Eastern spiritual practices. If your doctor/therapist/coach wants what is best for you, they will not try to force anything on you with which you are not comfortable. If they try to belittle or minimize your faith or ignore it completely, find someone new. They do not genuinely care about you. Also, finding a priest, especially one who is an expert in spirituality, with whom to consult is beneficial. They can help you sort out what to do and what not to do. They can assist you with explaining Catholic teaching to your doctor/therapist/coach.

As far as what practices to practice, a Catholic who wants to practice relaxation techniques, meditation, and mindfulness should be aware of the result of such practices. Do they bring you closer to God? Do they bring you peace? When there is uncertainty, talk with a priest. I would advise only practicing Catholic meditation. As far as mindfulness is concerned, the term itself has become a hotly debated topic among Catholics on the internet. When the term is not used, certain mindfulness-like practices seem acceptable. Being aware of the present moment and bringing God into it is exactly what Catholics ought to do. While I am not against mindfulness (at least as Bottaro defines it), I prefer to think of mindfulness-like practices I use as "awareness of mind, body, spirit, and environment." Human beings are body and spirit, and using our minds to be aware of both our bodies and spirits and how our current environment is affecting us in the present moment is using how God created us to bring us closer to Him. It is using God's creation to its fullest. God can speak to us in a variety of ways, and we need to be open to hearing His voice through a variety of mediums.

If any sniff of meditation or mindfulness is abhorrent to you, there are relaxation techniques that can help you relax in times of stress and anxiety. Relaxation will help you settle down and be open to hearing God in prayer. Relaxation is contradictory to stress and anxiety. The body cannot be relaxed and anxious at the same time. I have found that breathing exercises are helpful during moments of stress. Again, there are weird ones out there, but there is a simple one that can easily facilitate any prayer: Breathe deeply in, and then, breathe deeply out[185]. That is it. When I was taught this method, I was told to say a calming word or phrase as I breathed in and out. I immediately decided that, whenever I was to practice this,[186] I would use a prayer as my calming word or phrase. "Come Holy Spirit" or simply "Jesus" are excellent things to repeat as one breathes, especially if one wishes to use this breathing technique to prepare oneself for prayer or Mass. Another relaxation technique I use is deep muscle relaxation. This involves contracting one group of muscles as much as possible and then relaxing. You do this several times, starting with the facial muscles and working all the way throughout the body. By the time you get down to your feet, you will be relaxed. You might be skeptical about this technique. I was too when I first heard about it, but the first time I tried it, I was able to stop a downward spiral of negative thoughts and overthinking.

---

185   The rate at which you breathe is important. It can be helpful to have a guide for this. A person works best, as they can watch you to make sure you are doing it correctly. There are some videos or audio recordings on the internet. I use the app that came with my Apple Watch as my guide for this.

186   Which is far more seldom than it probably should be

The Power of the Pause

Honestly, one of the best practices I have learned in my training to become an ADHD coach for slowing down and approaching life in a calm and more mindful way is simply pausing. When studying to become an ADHD coach at the ADD Coach Academy, you encounter "The Power of the Pause" a lot. Simply put, it is taking a moment or two throughout your day to stop, maybe take a deep breath or two, and pay attention to that to which you are paying attention. When you do this frequently, you begin to do it instinctually, and you become more aware of the thoughts you have and how they could negatively impact you. Moreover, you are empowered to stop negative thoughts, combat false beliefs, and halt impulsive behavior that could harm you or others.

PRAYER TIPS*

"In praying, do not babble like the pagans, who think that they will be heard because of their many words." – Matthew 6:7

I Am Not a Prayer Expert

The heading "I Am Not a Prayer Expert" probably does not inspire confidence in a chapter called "Prayer Tips." However, I think it is an important warning for the reader. I do not want anyone to think I am some sort of prayer guru. It should be noted that I know next to nothing about prayer. The suggestions listed in the rest of this chapter are merely things that have helped me in my prayer life.[187] Perhaps, they might help you, but I offer no guarantees[188]. What is important is to find the prayer techniques and strategies that work best for you.

Step by Step

Large projects can often overwhelm those of us with ADHD. Looking at what seems to be an insurmountable task or what seems to be a lot of work can cause stress and/or inspire a seemingly uncontrollable urge to procrastinate.[189] One of the best pieces of advice ADHD experts have for tackling large tasks is to break the task into smaller chunks and take it step by step.

This can apply to one's spiritual life. The project of improving one's spiritual life is a daunting task. However, if one can break it down into smaller chunks, improving one's spiritual life can become easier and more manageable. For example, if you were to examine your prayer life and what is needed, you might find that a big step would be to simply start praying regularly. That may seem like that would be an adequate first step. However, it is not exactly clear how one establishes a regular prayer habit. You might need to break down this first step into smaller steps. You need to decide how long each day you should be praying, find time in your schedule (or make time) to pray,[190] find a place to pray, figure out what type of prayer you are going to try first,[191] and then actually start doing it. There is more to improving one's spiritual life than this, but this is simply an example of how to start breaking down the seemingly insurmountable task of improving one's spiritual life into small steps.

---

187   More or less

188   Please, do not ask the merchant from whom you bought this book for a refund if these strategies do not work for you. Also, if you find or have strategies that work better and are not listed in this book, let me know!

189   The answer to your question is: Yes, I did have to fight off a seemingly uncontrollable urge to procrastinate while writing this section.

190   You might even need to set an alarm or use some other reminder system to alert you that it is time to pray.

191   What method of prayer you are going to use is something you will have to examine and reexamine for the rest of your life.

Celebrate the Small Victories

As mentioned before, the ADHD brain craves dopamine. Activities that provide more frequent and easily obtainable rewards are more exciting and interesting to the ADHD brain than others. A person with ADHD can hack this trait and use it to their advantage. They can take a large task, break it down into small steps, and celebrate each time they accomplish a small step of the larger task. So, when a person with ADHD is attempting to improve their spiritual life and accomplishes one of their small steps, it is important to reward that good behavior. For example, if the ADHDer prays for fifteen minutes, they might reward that behavior by enjoying a bowl of ice cream.[192] Praying every day for a week might result in a trip to Amazon.com to buy something from their wishlist. Rewarding good prayer habits will help make those habits stick.

Relax

It is hard to prayer when overly excited. If you are angry or were just having a dance party before you start to pray, take some time to calm down before you attempt to pray. Take some deep breaths, or try relaxing all of your muscle groups one at a time. To relax your muscle groups, start with the face muscles, and work your way down to your toes. Contract the muscles in your face, hold it for a few seconds, and then relax. Repeat this a few times, and then move on to the other muscle groups. Whatever method you choose to calm yourself, make sure it that actually works for you and is not just something someone told you to do.

Sleep

Sleep is important. When the mind is tired, it rebels and refuses to pay attention. I know how hard it is to settle down at night and get to sleep,[193] but it is important. The snooze button is bad, and early bedtimes are good.[194] Without the requisite eight hours[195] of sleep we need each night, our prayer lives will suffer. It also a good idea to avoid signing up for late-night adoration shifts.[196] This will not only interfere with your prayer life during the holy hour but will also increase the severity of the struggles you face during the day in all areas of your life.

Aside from those mentioned above, the benefits of sleep are numerous. Getting enough sleep can prevent binge eating, make you a safer driver, prevent Alzheimer's, improve memory and learning, give you more energy, boost your immune system, prevent injuries, make you more creative, improve your ability to control your emotions,

---

192   It is not a good idea to consume high amounts of sugar every time you celebrate. It would behoove you to find healthy ways of celebrating. Although, there is nothing wrong with a little ice cream every once in a while.

193   To help myself fall asleep at night, I listen to a podcast called Sleep with Me. Yes, it has a scandalous title, but it is not sexual in nature. It is just a guy using a generally monotone voice to tell stories that are just interesting enough to get you to pay attention to the story instead of your racing thoughts, but not so interesting that it energizes you. And, to be clear, I am not being paid to promote this podcast in my book. I just am amazed at how much this podcast helps me fall asleep.

194   This is where everyone should point at me and shout, "Hypocrite! Hypocrite! Hypocrite!" I do not heed my own advice. I tell myself I will heed that advice, but do I? No. No, I do not.

195   Yes, you need eight hours of sleep each night. No, you are not the exception to this rule. Eight hours is what you need.

196   He wrote, speaking from personal experience.

help you perform better in all areas of life (including sports), and make you more attractive.[197]

Your Guardian Angel

Ask your guardian angel for help. Your guardian angel is always with you and is there for your benefit.[198] Take advantage of his aid. Ask him to help you focus your thoughts on prayer. He loves you! In fact, the only one who loves you more than your guardian angel is God.[199] Rejecting that kind of love is like rejecting the love of a puppy.

You can use the standard guardian angel prayer, but there are other options. You can also use your own words. Talk to him like he is a friend.[200] Saints have also composed their own guardian angel prayers. Here is a guardian prayer written by Saint Eugène de Mazenod:[201]

My good angel, my body may be here, but my heart is with God. You who are constantly at the foot of God's throne, offer him my intentions, tell him that I love him above all things. Amen.

The Palm Cross

It may sound counterintuitive, but making a palm cross actually helps me pay attention at Mass. Studies have shown that fidgeting helps ADHDers focus,[202] so when Palm Sunday rolls around, I get excited because the odds of me paying attention during Mass are significantly increased.[203] There are people on the internet who feel the act of making a palm cross is disrespectful and that we should pay attention at Mass. I counter with the scientifically valid assertion that the fidgeting improves concentration for some people, especially those with ADHD.

Fidget Toys

As I mentioned in the previous sections, scientists have found that fidgeting with something can improve the focus of those with ADHD. There is a growing market for fidget toys, and many are stepping up to claim a piece of that market share. I have tried a few of them and have mixed feelings about them.

The fidget cube was the first fidget toy to make a big splash on the internet.[204] This six-sided object has sever-

---

197   All of these benefits come from Why We Sleep: Unlocking the Power of Sleep and Dreams by Matthew Walker, PhD

198   He is there for your benefit alone. Guardian angels do not pull double duty and are not recycled (The non-recycling of guardian angels is difficult to prove in a small amount of space. Suffice it to say that, when you think about angels, remember that they exist outside of time). The only soul your guardian angel is charged with protecting and guiding is your own. Take advantage of that!

199   Although, there are some who say Mary loves you more than your guardian angel does. My point is: The list of individuals who love you more than your guardian angel does is short.

200   After all, he is your friend. At least, he should be.

201   Saint Eugène wrote this prayer for his sister to use in times of temptation.

202   More on that in the next section

203   However, my palm cross skills have increased to the point where my palm cross is finished before the gospel, leaving me with well over half the Mass left without a palm cross to make.

204   Just to make sure I do not get a bunch of people writing me angry letters, I want to be clear: The fidget cube was the first fidget toy I

al different fidgets one can do with it to help one concentrate. Some of them are fun. Others are less so. Sometimes, the effectiveness of the fidget depends on how well the cube was manufactured. The fidget cube was marketed as an object that can be easily hidden in one's pocket and is a quiet way to fidget without disturbing others. I have found both of those to be untrue. The cube I have bulges out of my pocket, and it is obvious I have a fidget cube in my pocket.[205] Furthermore, it fails to meet the quiet standard it set for itself in its marketing. Some of the fidgets do, in fact, make noise. This kills its potential to be used in church, school, work, movie theaters, etc. I have also purchased a 12-sided fidget cube[206] which has some of the same fidgets and some new ones but also omits some others. The pros and cons of this 12-sided fidget toy are the same as the six-sided fidget cube. The best part of the 12-sided fidget toy was the instructions which were hilariously translated into English from Chinese.

The fidget spinner craze has turned many off to spinners. However, many people find them useful. There is a Buzzfeed video of people with ADHD and anxiety trying fidget spinners for a week. A good number of them gained no benefits from using the spinner, but there are people in that video who grew to love their spinner by the end of the week. I know a few people with ADHD who like the fidget spinner, but based on my observations, it is more useful for people who have anxiety. Personally, I fail to see how holding a spinner while it spins is considered fidgeting and helps one with the urge to fidget. However, I will say it is quieter than the fidget cube. Yet, the spinning action makes it distracting to anyone else in the room.

The flippy chain is my favorite fidget toy. I am not exactly sure how to describe what it is. It has two metal rings, and there are two pieces of metal which attach to one side of each ring. With one hand, you flip the pieces of metal around. It sounds lame, but it feels great. If you buy the right one, it is quiet and fits easily into your pocket.[207]

Movement

You are allowed to move as you pray. Too often, prayer is seen as a rigid activity. However, there is no reason why one cannot pace or walk about a room as one prays. Yet, this action might distract others if you do this around other people.[208] Pay attention to your circumstances, and know how you will be expected to behave in each scenario in which you find yourself.

There also multiple postures that one can assume during prayer. One can stand, sit, kneel, or lie prostrate while praying. I also see no reason why a person could not pace while praying. One can satisfy one's need to move while praying by switching up one's prayer posture as the desire arises. However, at certain times (e.g. during Mass),

---

saw creating a lot of buzz on the internet. The spinner or another fidget toy may have made it big first, but I did not notice that.

205   And, I am a guy. I cannot imagine what the cube looks like when it is in those ridiculously small pockets they put on women's pants.

206   A cube with 12 sides is not a cube, but I do not know what else to call it. Plus, it is marketed as a cube, which makes me a little bit sad.

207   Yes, it works for your pockets, too, ladies!

208   If you would prefer to not have others distract you while you are trying to pray, be mindful of others while they are praying and offer them the same courtesy.

certain postures are expected of you.[209] Be sure to follow those customs when it is expected of you, but when you have the opportunity to freely choose your prayer posture, do whatever works best for you.

Furthermore, one's daily exercise routine can incorporate spiritual exercise along with physical exercises. There is no getting around it; exercise is boring. Adding prayer into the mix might make things more stimulating or at least less monotonous. There is a group called the Life Runners that prays for the unborn while running. There are also exercise videos you can buy that leads you in both the prayer and yoga[210] exercises.[211] By the way, gentlemen, I hear the ladies really dig "Rosary walks."[212] Also, praying while exercising is a great way to sanctify one's workout and perhaps create an opportunity to reflect on how our bodies are temples of the Holy Spirit[213] and our duty to care for that temple.

Pray Out Loud

I (and others) have found that praying out loud helps keep prayer on track. Obviously, this is not recommended when praying out loud would be a nuisance to others. However, if you are alone or praying a Rosary with a group, praying out loud can[214] work wonders.

Use a Prayer Journal

Writing in a prayer journal helps me organize my prayer into coherent thoughts.[215] I can explain the consolations and the desolations I receive in prayer. Also, I have found using my prayer journal to write letters to the Lord (especially during times of stress) to be an effective and powerful method of prayer. Furthermore, my prayer sometimes takes the form of writing poetry.[216] I have found my prayer journal to be an excellent place for composing those poems.

Prayer journals do not have to be anything special. There is no need to buy a leather notebook with an attached ribbon bookmark.[217] Got to a store and buy the cheapest notebook you can find. Or, find an old notebook

---

209   Those who selected those postures had good reasons for doing so. If you do some research on those choices, I think you will agree with me on that.

210   Yoga is another one of those fads that has eastern roots. Stretching and core-strengthening exercises are good for the body, but if one is not careful, some yoga instructions could lead to practicing some eastern spiritual practices that can lead down a dark path.

211   I have found, though, that I spent most of the time wondering if I was doing the exercises right rather than focusing on prayer.

212   You're welcome.

213   Yes, I know how over-used and cheesy that expression is, but it nevertheless expresses a profound truth. God gave us our bodies as a gift, and God dwells in each one of us. Therefore, no matter how cheesy it sounds, our bodies are temples of the Holy Spirit.

214   Note: I said, "can" and not "will." It might not work for you, and that is okay as long as you keep striving to improve your spiritual life and find what works best for your prayer life.

215   More or less

216   Some of these poems have been published. Check out *Poems I Found in My Prayer Journals* on Amazon. Note: If you read them, do not expect them to be of high quality.

217   I have one of those for writing poetry (not the poetry that winds up in my prayer journal, mind you). This special poetry notebook does not impress the ladies like I expected it would.

from school[218] that has a good number of unused pages left. If you rip out those notes you never look at anymore,[219] you have a perfect notebook for beginning your prayer journal.

I have never done it, but it is entirely acceptable to take notes in your prayer journal during the homily. If you are willing to have people look at you funny, go ahead and try it.[220] Taking notes will also help with the "I really liked Father's homily today. Wait, what was it about again?" problem.

The Jesus Prayer

The Jesus prayer is a simple prayer that can be said periodically throughout the day to keep the presence of Christ in mind as we go about our daily lives. This prayer, which has ancient origins,[221] is popular in the Orthodox Church and is sometimes prayed on beads.[222] The prayer usually takes the formula: "Lord Jesus Christ, Son of God, have mercy on me, a sinner." However, Doctor Peter Kreeft[223] says the Jesus prayer is simply saying the name Jesus. Regardless of what the Jesus prayer actually is or can be, the important thing is what it accomplishes. The Jesus prayer is a simple prayer that can be said at any time of the day to remind the one praying it of the presence of Jesus at any time of the day.

Write a List of Things to Not Think About

Write out a list of things that are on your mind before you start praying. Take this list, offer it up to the Lord, and then set it aside. Sometimes this works, but more often than not, it causes me to become even more distracted.[224] I liken this strategy's problems to the old "Don't think about elephants" routine. What do you end up thinking about? You end up thinking about elephants. When I have written a list of things not think about while praying, not only do I keep thinking about those things, but I find myself adding more things to that list and thinking about even more things I should not be. In short, I consider this to be the least reliable method for staying focused during prayer, but I have included it because others discuss it and there is a chance it might work for you.[225]

One thing that has worked for me is having a paper and a pen nearby while praying. When a distracting thought or an idea comes to me that I want to address later, I write it down. This way, I am not even more distracted by hoping I remember the thought or idea that just popped into my head.

---

218   My first prayer journal used to be an advanced chemistry notebook.

219   Covalent bonds? Psh! Who needs 'em?!

220   The looks are the main reason I have not tried it.

221   It can be traced back to the fourth century according to a website I found that looked totally legitimate. You can always tell a website is legitimate when it looks like it was designed in the 1990s. On a completely unrelated note, why has no one invented a font that conveys sarcasm?

222   Those who pray it on beads are almost always monks.

223   One of my favorite authors. Look him up.

224   I think this strategy for staying focused during prayer was invented by someone without ADHD.

225   Experimentation is key in finding effective strategies for coping with ADHD.

Missal

To help me focus during Mass, I use a missal,[226] a book that has all of the prayers and readings of the Mass. I have found seeing the words that are spoken during the Mass helps me stay on top of what is happening. I do still lose my place, but the act of trying to find out where the priest is in the liturgy helps me get back on track. There is something about flipping around that book that helps me stay in touch with what is going on during the Mass. Additionally, using a missal has the added benefit of helping a person learn the Mass and the various parts therein.[227]

Pray with Scripture

Do not just read scripture; pray with scripture. Reading a passage from the Bible, especially the Psalms, gives you something to meditate upon during prayer. Look into Lectio[228] Divina, a method of praying with scripture taught by St. Ignatius of Loyola. Lectio Divina allows a person to lose himself/herself in scripture. In some sense, the mind is allowed to wander as one reflects on a small piece of scripture.

There are five steps to Lectio Divina.[229] The first step is called "Lectio." Here the selection of scripture is read, preferably more than once. The second step, "Meditatio," involves meditating on what was just read, sometimes focusing[230] or reflecting on a word or phrase that sticks out[231] to the one who is praying. Next, the third step, "Oratio," invites the person praying to pray with the passages that have captured their attention. The fourth step, "Contemplatio," is the hardest. It involves contemplating the truths that God has revealed in this time of prayer. Lastly, the final step, "Actio," invites the person praying to take what they received in prayer and apply it to one's life. As a final note on Lectio Divina, it is perfectly acceptable to re-read the scripture passage in between each step (and I would encourage you to do so).

Switch It Up

Once, while confessing my lack of focus in prayer and at Mass,[232] a priest warned me to be careful about what I was saying. He told me that, sometimes, God allows us to be distracted in prayer because He wants us to try a different method of prayer. This might not always be true, but in this instance, I believe he was right. My prayer

---

226   It is not the same thing as a missile. It is a book, not a weapon. However, it feels pretty B.A. to call it a missal.

227   I was recently asked for a missal recommendation for someone who is in the process of converting. She had no background understanding of the Mass but wanted to participate more when she attends Mass. I sent a long video detailing all of the contents of my missal. It was probably far too long because I was super excited to share this with her due to the great benefit my missal has been for me.

228   "Lectio" is pronounced "leck-see-oh." I once listened to an audio recording of a famous Catholic speaker about this method of prayer, and he kept calling it "Leck-tee-oh" Divina. I kept wanting to scream at him, "You're saying it wrong!" He had a great message, but I could not get over his mispronunciation.

229   I am not an expert in Ignatian spirituality. This explanation might be subpar, but it should be enough to get you started. If you would like a better description of Lectio Divina, there are many resources available online.

230   As best as one can

231   I once had a powerful prayer experience about feet while praying Lectio Divina.

232   This was prior to my ADHD diagnosis, mind you.

life was not the best at that point in time, and the method of prayer I was using at the time was ineffective. I needed to hit the reset button on my spiritual life.[233]

When you are struggling to pray, do not be afraid to try other methods of prayer. There is a reason God gave us many methods of prayer. He wants His children to have options when it comes to prayer. Lectio Divina is not for everyone. Not everyone should pray the Rosary.[234] Only certain people are called to pray litanies every day.[235]

It is important to find that method of prayer that works best for you. When someone encourages you to do a particular prayer method, ask them why they think that prayer method would work best for you. They will probably respond with some general information about that method of praying and/or with their own personal experience. At that time, you should remind them that you wanted to know what it was about that prayer method that would be fitting for your prayer life, not theirs.[236]

Persevere

The most important thing a person with ADHD can do for their prayer life is to persevere. Nothing I mentioned above is a surefire method for overcoming ADHD while praying, but it is important to never give up. The Lord knows that you did not choose ADHD, so He understands your struggle to focus. God still loves you, no matter what. The key is to keep trying.[237] I once again[238] remind you of the words of Saint Francis de Sales:

> If the heart wanders or is distracted, bring it back to the point quite gently and replace it tenderly in its
> Master's presence. And even if you did nothing during the whole of your hour but bring your heart back
> and place it again in Our Lord's presence, though it went away every time you brought it back, your hour
> would be very well employed.

---

233   "If you want to hit the reset button on your ADHD, visit ResetADHD.com," he wrote with a substantial amount of bias.

234   Although, there are some who will tell you otherwise. Yes, Marian devotion is extremely powerful, and I highly recommend it. However, it is not a sin to not pray the Rosary or not seek the intercession of the saints. The only method of prayer that is not optional is the Mass.

235   I like litanies, but the repetitiveness of it gets monotonous, which makes it hard for me to pay attention.

236   Yes, dear reader, I can, indeed, hear you sarcastically saying, "Gee, Alex, have you had people try to force their opinions on you with regards to what you should and should not do?"

237   The foundation of holiness, in my humble opinion, is the decision to try to be holy. (I am sure there is a saint quote somewhere that will refute that.)

238   Or, I am telling you about this quote for the first time if you skipped the chapter on shame.

WHERE DO YOU PRAY?

"[W]hen you pray, go to your inner room, close the door, and pray to your Father in secret. And your Father who sees in secret will repay you." – Matthew 6:6

Location, Location, Location

The first three rules of real estate also apply to prayer. I do not recommend praying in a football stadium, surrounded by thousands of screaming fans.[239] That will not work. Neither is praying in your bedroom a good idea. The bedroom is where you sleep. Your brain knows, when it is on the bed, it is where it gets to rest. To pray in one's bedroom is to invite the temptation to sleep instead of pray.

There are many excellent places to pray. The place where I can best focus on praying is the presence of the Eucharist. There is something about praying in the presence of the Blessed Sacrament that draws me into prayer more deeply than anywhere else.[240] Furthermore, I have had some fantastic prayer experiences in nature, specifically in the White Tank Mountains in Arizona.[241] It can be beneficial to pray someplace that provides a beautiful view, even if that view is an urban setting. This could be on the balcony of a tall apartment building, or it could be on the roof[242] of a tall building.[243] Also, there is something to be said for designating a place to pray in one's home. When I moved into my current townhouse, I gained a small loft space that I turned into a prayer nook. You might not have room for that in your house, so be on the lookout for quiet, secluded places that can be your prayer zone. A walk-in closet might even be an option. It is best, though, to find a place with images that will draw your attention to the sacred. Speaking of which…

Images

One of the best strategies I have to keep myself focused during prayer is engaging as many senses as possible. Having sacred images near me is probably the most effective way of engaging one of my senses to keep me

---

239   Trust me. God doesn't care if your favorite team wins or not. If He did, the Vikings would have won the Super Bowl by now.

240   For those non-ADHDers who are thinking, *Well, duh! Of course, you are going to be more focused in the presence of Jesus*, I should remind you that ADHDers cannot choose when to focus. We cannot choose to focus just because something is important or special to us. Yes, it is more likely that we will be able to focus better on those things which interest us the most, but that is far from a reliable means of predicting how well we will focus.

241   Your nature preferences might be different from mine.

242   Remember when I discussed climbing buildings in a footnote in the chapter "What Is ADHD?" Those climbing experiences led to a powerful experience while praying the Rosary near the top of the tallest building on my new campus under the stars and gazing upon the blue lights of a nearby hospital.

243   For legal reasons, I should probably point out that climbing buildings is most likely illegal and could result in serious injury. Perhaps, find a safer way to find a beautiful view.

focused on prayer. A person cannot always find a place with beautiful images surrounding them in which to pray. In these instances, it behooves one to have some sacred images on display. Find a crucifix or a painting of Mary. Praying with images such as these can help redirect oneself when distractions arise. If you find yourself becoming distracted, look at those images to bring yourself back into prayer. If the place you have designated as your prayer area is not decorated with sacred images, keep some prayer cards in your prayer journal or Bible and set them out during your prayer time.

Where to Attend Mass

The importance of location and images is why it is important to attend Mass in a beautiful church. The first time I attend Mass at Saint Paul's Cathedral in Saint Paul, Minnesota, I had no issues staying focused on the sacred. I abhor parishes that decorate their worship space more like a non-denominational church than a church built in medieval Europe.[244] I consider myself blessed to live in the same city[245] as the magnificent Saint Joseph's Cathedral.[246] A well-decorated church will be filled with stain glass windows, statues, and other forms of sacred art that draw people into the mystery of what is occurring during the Mass.

---

244   I am really tempted to name names here.

245   Sioux Falls, SD

246   Shout out to Bishop Paul Swain for the work he did to get our Cathedral restored to reflect the original intentions of the architect (the same architect who designed St. Paul's Cathedral, by the way).

HOW DOES GOD SPEAK TO YOU?

"Were not our hearts burning [within us] while He spoke to us on the way and opened the scriptures to us?" – Luke 24:32

Sit Still, Be Quiet, Listen, Be Patient, and Other Things ADHDers Struggle to Do

When prayer is discussed, four of the most common recommendations are: Sit still, be quiet, listen, and be patient. All of these appear to be steps one needs to take before learning and understanding God's will. These are all excellent suggestions…for neurotypicals.

The ADHD brain works differently from typical brains. Therefore, those with ADHD will need to pray differently. Advice telling us to sit still, be quiet, listen, and be patient does us no good. We struggle to sit still. Our minds only grow quiet when we finally are able to fall asleep. We can often hear without listening. Patience is also not our strong suit.

You Are Unique

We all hear a lot of advice on prayer, discernment, and listening for God's voice. In my personal experience, though, not much of that advice has actually helped me. The people who share this wisdom are smart, holy people, and the tips they give are neither heretical nor illogical. Their tips just do not seem to work for me. Should these people stop giving advice on listening to God's voice? No, but readers and/or listeners of theirs should be aware that everyone is unique and, therefore, hears the voice of God in a unique way. For example, there is a priest in my diocese who says God speaks to him through the language of nerd.[247] Not everyone has that unusual of a way of hearing God speak to them, but everyone does have their own unique method. It is imperative that each and every one of us take the time to figure out what that is.

Round up the Usual Suspects![248]

How, though, do you begin to determine the unique way in which God speaks to you? Well, one method is to experiment with the usual ways of hearing God's voice. The Bible is God's word, so there is a good chance there is something in there that might speak to you. You could also follow that trite piece of advice that is a common suggestion given by alleged experts in prayer: Step away from the noise of everyday life.[249] Furthermore, priests are

---

247   He has a very specific and unorthodox definition of what "nerd" means, so he is not making the claim that God speaks to him through comic books.

248   +10 points if you caught the reference.

249   My response to that advice is, "Then, what?"

called to be Christ's representatives. Hopefully, one can hear God speak through their homilies and the other ways they share their priestly wisdom.

The voice of God might even come outside of prayer. While the traditional method of hearing His voice is through prayer, there are no limits to how God can speak to us. He is all-powerful and will speak to us however He darn well pleases. The beauty of nature speaks to certain people. Others have reported that music is a way God speaks to them. Saint Thérèse of Lisieux believed that God does not always speak through prayer and wrote about how she heard the voice of God:

> I know and have experienced that 'the Kingdom of God is within us,' that our Master has no need of books or teacher to instruct a soul. The Teacher of teachers instructs without sound of words, and though I have never heard Him speak, yet I know He is within me, always guiding and inspiring me; and just when I need them, lights, hitherto unseen, break in upon me. As a rule, it is not during prayer that this happens, but in the midst of my daily duties.

God speaks to us in everyday life, and we need to be on alert in order to hear how he speaks to us. Our interactions with loved ones or even strangers can be an instance of God speaking to us. Sometimes, God intercedes in our life to make a point. He might give you a grace or a blessing to awaken you to His voice. God can also allow a suffering[250] in your life to open a channel to you. As Venerable[251] Fulton Sheen said, "Sometimes, the only way the good Lord can enter into some hearts is to break them." A tragedy can be the voice of God calling you, or it could be God knocking you off your high horse.[252]

Relax! It Is Not Easy

While preparing to write this chapter, I read an article online with the headline, "It's Not That Complicated."[253] My initial instinct after reading that headline was to flip off the author, but I did not because A.) that is not a nice thing to do and B.) she could not see me. I was angry because I know from years of experience that it is difficult to learn how God speaks to you. He may also speak to you in different ways at different times in your life. It is complicated and will not be easy.[254] Do not allow yourself to feel stressed if you are unsure of how God speaks to you. It will take time to learn, and that is okay.

---

250   Perhaps ADHD?

251   Soon to be Blessed

252   That literally happened to Saint Paul in Acts 9:3-4.

253   I learned nothing from it and do not recommend it.

254   Unless you are Saint Pio of Pietrelcina who, when he was a young child, thought everyone could see Jesus, Mary, and their guardian angel because that is how natural prayer was for him.

You Know It When You Hear It

The desire for God is written on our hearts. "Our hearts are restless until they rest in [God]," as Saint Augustine would say. Therefore, when we encounter the voice of God, there are signs found in our hearts that indicate what we have just heard is God speaking to us. The voice of God brings joy and peace. What we feel when we think God is trying to tell us something should bring us joy, not anxiety. That sense of feeling satisfied in one's heart is a good indication of the Lord's voice. However, God is not always direct and may speak more subtly. In these instances, more prayerful meditation on what we think God might be saying is needed. Talking things over with a loved one and/or a spiritual advisor is also of great benefit.

SAINTS FOR ADHD

"I know that this will result in deliverance for me through your prayers and support from the Spirit of Jesus Christ." – Philippians 1:19

Why Do We Need This Chapter?

The example and intercession of the saints can be of tremendous benefit in all areas of our life, but especially in the area where we need the most help.[255] In that area, we want to find a saint like us, that struggled with the same things we do, yet overcame those struggles to become holy. This thought was most eloquently expressed by Pope Paul VI:

> We want to discover in saints whatever brings them closer to us, rather than what sets them apart. We want to put them at our level as human beings…That way, we stand the chance of having confidence in them – we can share with them the common and burdensome state of our earthly experience.

There have been no saints who have been diagnosed with ADHD[256]. While we wait for the Church to canonize someone with documented ADHD,[257] we must find those saints who struggled with the same sorts of things that affect those of us with ADHD. Below I have compiled a list of some saints I think could be powerful intercessors for those of us who have ADHD.

Saint Anthony of Padua

The namesake of San Antonio, Texas, Saint Anthony of Padua is often asked for his intercession when lost items cannot be found. Those with ADHD lose stuff all the time. It is a no-brainer to keep him in mind when seeking an intercessor for struggles related to ADHD.

Saint Dymphna

Saint Dymphna was killed by her father who had slipped into mental illness following the death of his wife, Dymphna's mother. Her father wanted to marry her because she looked so much like her deceased mother. She fled to what is now known as Geel, Belgium where he eventually found her and killed her.

---

255   I am willing to bet for many of you reading this book that the area where you need it the most is in dealing with either your ADHD or that of a loved one's.

256   Although, I think there is a possibility Saint Thomas Aquinas had ADHD, and as you will see, it is incredibly likely that St. Joseph of Cupertino had it.

257   Perhaps, it will be you!

A church named after her was built in 1349. Within one hundred years of the church's erection, it became known as a place where the mentally ill could find care, and some found miraculous cures. To this day, those seeking mental health care flock to Geel, and the townspeople welcome them into their homes because the mental health facilities there are always at capacity. This has led her to become the patron saint of mental illness and other mental-health-related issues.

Saint Eugène de Mazenod

While in exile during the French Revolution, thirteen-year-old Saint Eugène de Mazenod's parents separated. He tried several times to reunite them, but he was never successful. Because of the trials he suffered in his family life, Saint Eugène was declared by Pope Saint John Paul II to be the patron saint of dysfunctional families or families in crisis.

Yet, one of the strange things one discovers while studying the life of Saint Eugène de Mazenod is the lack of information available on how the pain of his parents' divorce affected him. His writings hardly mention it. The book *Eugène de Mazenod: A Saint for Today*[258] asserts that the reason he did not write more about his parents' divorce and the pains it caused him was that Saint Eugène recognized that he is more than the child of divorced parents. He is not a child of divorced parents; he is a beloved son of God who happens to have divorced parents.

When the life of Saint Eugène de Mazenod is examined, it is clear that he lived his life believing he had dignity because of who his Heavenly Father is. This is how those of us with ADHD ought to view ourselves. We are not screw-ups or hyperactive freaks; we are beloved children of God who happen to have ADHD. We are not defined by ADHD. We "are God's children, the brothers of Jesus Christ, heirs to His eternal kingdom, chosen portion of His inheritance." [259]

Saint John Vianney

Saint John Vianney was thought to lack intelligence. His academic struggles almost doomed his chances of becoming a priest. His piety convinced his superiors to overlook his academic shortcomings and allow Saint John Vianney to be ordained to the priesthood. He soon became known as one of the best confessors in the world.

Saint John Vianney tried his best in school, but his test scores were unsatisfactory. Yet, his expertise in the confessional prove that he did not lack knowledge of theology and spirituality; he simply did not do well in an academic environment. This is where those with ADHD can find comfort. Even if our efforts to succeed in school or other areas of life fail, we can still look to Saint John Vianney as an example of someone who was successful, despite academic failure.

---

258   OK, you caught me! I wrote *Eugène de Mazenod: A Saint for Today*. Did I include Saint Eugène in this list so I could promote my other book? Not entirely. I would be tickled pink if you bought my book, but I strongly feel that Saint Eugène is a powerful example of recognizing our true dignity as children of God and not being defined by the tragedies of our lives.

259   From Saint Eugène's 1813 Ash Wednesday sermon

Saint Joseph of Cupertino[260]

Saint Joseph of Cupertino[261] had nothing going for him early in life. Aside from being born into a family with financial difficulties, he was frequently ill. Joseph was also absent-minded and unable to hold a conversation or tell a story from start to finish. He was so easily distracted that he could sometimes forget to eat.[262] His issues with focus prevented him from completing school, and he was apprenticed as a shoemaker after leaving school. His lack of focus doomed his apprenticeship as well. The struggles Joseph had with things most everyone could handle with ease caused him to be rejected by everyone, including his own mother. This led him to think poorly about himself.

At the age of seventeen, he saw a friar enter his village and begin begging, and Joseph decided that was something he might actually be able to do. Several orders rejected him because of his lack of schooling. When one finally accepted him, he was shortly thereafter dismissed because he would get swept up in pious thoughts and abstractions. This would occur even when he was doing some chore which, on one occasion, caused him to drop and break several plates.

Joseph would later refer to the day he was dismissed from the order as the worst day of his life. After a long and tumultuous walk home, Joseph arrived back at his parents' home and received no sympathy. His mother chewed him out for being expelled from a religious order and refused to let him stay in her home. She went to her brother who was a high-ranking member of the Franciscan order that had expelled Joseph and begged him to take him off of her hands. Refusing to let him be a Franciscan friar, Joseph's uncle and the Franciscans reluctantly allowed Joseph to take the habit of a lay brother and assigned him to the stable to care for the monastery's mule.

Riddled with self-doubt, Joseph accepted his assignment and figured it was all he was worth. He embraced his lowliness and became an extraordinarily happy and friendly friar. The other Franciscans took notice and decided to give him another chance to become a priest. Still, Joseph struggled to learn and was only able to excel at expounding upon one scripture passage. Despite his poor academic performance, he managed to make it through his preparations for the priesthood to the point of an examination by his bishop for his fitness for ordination to the diaconate. When it was his turn, the bishop opened up the Bible and pointed to a random scripture passage and asked Joseph to explain it. By God's providence, it was that one scripture passage which he could discuss at length. The bishop consented to his ordination to the diaconate. A year later, Joseph needed to be examined again in order to be ordained to the priesthood. He waited as he and his classmates were each individually questioned. After the first few candidates were interviewed, the bishop was so impressed that he approved the ordination of everyone in the class.

After ordination, Joseph continued to live with humility and joy. Episodes where he would be swept into

---

260   I am going to have to try really hard to resist the urge to talk about how he is the patron saint of astronauts, which is freaking awesome.

261   Fun fact: I have chosen Saint Joseph of Cupertino as the patron of my coaching practice, Reset ADHD.

262   Something to which many ADHDers can relate.

abstractions continued, and people began to notice his piety and how he would sometimes levitate during these periods of ecstasy. His superiors thought that this drew too much attention to him, and for thirty-five years, he was barred from public ministry. For someone who was ordained in his early twenties and would only live to the age of sixty, this period of seclusion accounted for basically the entirety of his priesthood.

Saint Joseph of Cupertino's story is an example of someone who could not concentrate on his studies and hyperfocused on God. Despite his struggles living a normal life, he was able to live a life of heroic virtue. Saint Joseph of Cupertino is probably the closest we have ever come to knowing of a saint who had ADHD.[263]

Saint Monica

This one is more for parents of children with ADHD. At times, parents of children with ADHD suffer greatly because of the challenges of raising children with ADHD.[264] In moments of distress over the care of a child with ADHD, I encourage parents to turn to Saint Monica.

Saint Monica is the mother of Saint Augustine, one of the Church's greatest saints and also one of the greatest scoundrels. Augustine made life miserable for his mother. Before becoming a priest (and later Bishop of Hippo), Saint Augustine embraced a pagan lifestyle, publicly defied Christian doctrine, and fathered a child out of wedlock. Throughout the many years of Augustine's sinful lifestyle, Monica never ceased praying for the conversion of her son.[265] Her dedication to praying for her troublesome child should be an inspiration to parents everywhere.

Saint Thérèse of Lisieux

Saint Thérèse of Lisieux knew suffering well. If one even skims her autobiography, it becomes impossible to deny she was well acquainted with suffering. Most of her sufferings came from deaths in her family and her many health problems. One of the sufferings people tend to neglect when exploring and/or explaining her difficult life is the struggles she endured in prayer. In *Story of a Soul*, she writes, "I have many distractions, but as soon as I am aware of them, I pray for those people, the thought of whom is diverting my attention. In this way, they reap the benefit of my distractions." One of her most significant sources of struggle was the Rosary:

> [W]hen alone (I am ashamed to admit it) the recitation of the Rosary is more difficult for me than the wearing of an instrument of penance...I force myself in vain to meditate on the mysteries of the Rosary; I don't succeed in fixing my mind on them.

> For a long time, I was desolate about this lack of devotion which astonished me, for I love the Blessed Virgin so much that it should be easy for me to recite in her honor prayers which are so pleasing to her. Now I

---

263   ADHD has been around for a long time, but only recently has it come to the attention of the general public. It is entirely likely that there has been a saint (or perhaps many saints) who suffered from ADHD and could not get diagnosed because there were no diagnostic criteria then. Also, there are saints we do not know about. So, hypothetically speaking, there could be many saints in Heaven right now who did have an ADHD diagnosis, and God has not willed for them to be canonized and thereby publicly recognized by the Church as a saint.

264   But, it is not the child's fault that they have ADHD. If you have ADHD, fret not! You are not to blame for your parents' suffering.

265   Her prayers were also responsible for the conversion of her pagan husband.

am less desolate; I think that the Queen of Heaven, since she is my mother, must see my good will and she is satisfied with it.

In exploring the life of the Little Flower, it is imperative to remember her struggles in prayer. People often point to the attitude with which she suffered her emotional and physical trials, but the most amazing aspect of her struggles was how she endured them despite her inability to focus as well as she would have liked.

Saint Thomas Aquinas

Called "The Dumb Ox" in school by both his fellow students and his teachers, Saint Thomas Aquinas was thought to be quite stupid by his schoolmates. When he attended lectures, he rarely spoke up, leading his peers to think he was struggling in school. One of his classmates offered to tutor him out of pity. To avoid hurting his classmate's feelings, Thomas agreed to be tutored. During the lesson, the wannabe tutor reached a difficult section and was baffled when "The Dumb Ox" explained it perfectly to him.

A common misconception about those with ADHD is that we are not smart individuals. The truth of the matter is ADHD affects people of all levels of intelligence. In fact, there is a great number of ADHDers who are extremely intelligent.[266] When faced with suggestions, either from others or within ourselves, that we are dumb, lazy, or otherwise not good enough, we can ask for the intercession of Saint Thomas Aquinas to bring us comfort.

---

266   I, for one, was surprised when, during the process of getting my ADHD diagnosis, I learned into what percentile my IQ score fell.

SHARED BROKENNESS

"For where two or three are gathered together in My name, there am I in the midst of them." – Matthew 18:20

You Are Not Alone

If you are reading this book because you have ADHD, I bring you tidings of great joy: You are not alone. There are others out there like you. We can struggle together, and that is beautiful.

The "Palmer" Family

My senior year of high school, I began attending a retreat for high school and college students that is held in my diocese three times per year. I live in Sioux Falls, South Dakota, which has a population of around 250,000 in the metro statistical area. However, most towns in the state of South Dakota have much smaller populations. When members of the Catholic Diocese of Sioux Falls gather, the city folk end up meeting a lot of people from small, farming communities. It can be a culture shock at times. This introverted city slicker has had an especially hard time interacting with these people. For years, I knew of a family, the "Palmers," who attended all three of these retreats every year, so I was forced to interact with the Palmers many times. I never found much common ground with them despite knowing them for years.

After attending these retreats for a couple of years, I was diagnosed with ADHD, which sent me on a path of self-discovery. As I began learning more about myself and studying ADHD, I began to feel passionate about talking about ADHD; whereas, I previously kept my ADHD diagnosis private. This led to me discovering that the matriarch of the Palmer family also has ADHD, as does all four of her children.[267] When I discovered that this family I knew from retreats and with whom I never interacted much also had ADHD, my attitude towards them changed. I began to understand them better, and their odd quirks became indicative of the fact that they have ADHD, not that they are country bumpkins. As I saw more of myself in them, I saw more of Christ in them. I now consider the matriarch of the Palmer family someone on whom I can rely for intelligent and heartfelt conversations. We have had many heart-to-heart conversations since I made this realization.[268]

---

267   I am not sure how this discovery was made. I cannot imagine it came up randomly in conversation. The only thing I can think of is the fact that I wrote an article for EpicPew.com about being a Catholic with ADHD. However, I feel like I knew they also had ADHD before I wrote that article. Who knows? I suppose it is not that important.

268   She is full of wisdom. Take, for example, this gem she sent me in a Facebook message: "People can relate to flaws - and they fear perfection in others - as the most perfect human to walk the earth was crucified." BOOM!

Come Together[269]

Human beings were not made for isolation. We are meant to live in community. The phrase "No man is an island," while trite, still reflects a great truth. The human person needs others.[270] You do not have to struggle with ADHD on your own; you are not alone.

Because you are not alone, do not be afraid to talk about having ADHD. There is nothing of which to be ashamed. Find others who also have ADHD and discuss your struggles and the things you do to manage your ADHD. These interactions will inspire you to try even harder to get your ADHD under control.

---

269   My apologies for getting a song by The Beatles stuck in your head!

270   As an introvert, I cringe while writing this, but it is true.

STRENGTHS

"As each one has received a gift, use it to serve one another as good stewards of God's varied grace. Whoever preaches, let it be with the words of God; whoever serves, let it be with the strength that God supplies, so that in all things God may be glorified through Jesus Christ, to Whom belong glory and dominion forever and ever. Amen." – 1 Peter 4:10-11

The Secret to Success When One Has ADHD

Those of us with ADHD have faults. Most of the time, we know our weaknesses. We have been told of our failings time and time again. However, being told about our faults is not what inspires us to better our lives. What does is identifying and developing our strengths. Doctors Edward Hallowell and John Ratey, leading experts in ADHD lament in their book, Delivered from Distraction, that, when a person is diagnosed with ADHD, they are only told what is wrong with them. Hallowell and Ratey want those with ADHD to know they do have strengths and that is where the focus should be.

Identifying Strengths

To identify one's strengths is not easy. As I write this section, I find myself wondering, What are my strengths? How does one discover one's talents? Am I even qualified to write about identifying and developing one's strengths? There are tests one can take and books one can buy to help identify one's strengths. If those work for you, great! Explore them all you want. But, if you are like me, you find those tests monotonous and those books preachy or missing something. In which case, I advise you to pay attention to the compliments others give you.[271] In what areas of your life do people give you words of affirmation? Do not focus on the negative. Pay attention to when others acknowledge things you have done well, and embrace the compliment. Due to the mistakes those with ADHD commonly make, those of us with ADHD often expect criticism and dwell on our faults, and when we do receive a compliment, it is easy to ignore it, knowing at any moment we could screw up again.

There are also several areas where it is quite common for those with ADHD to excel. Many ADHDers are creative. The areas of art, writing, acting, and music are loaded with ADHDers leading the way. We might not be able to succeed in school or at an office job, but we can dominate in the fine arts. Furthermore, we make great inventors.[272] We think not only outside the box, but we also think outside the room in which the box is located. When it comes to crunch time or crisis mode, ADHDers thrive. If you want something done last minute, find someone with

---

271   "What compliments do people give me?" is a question I asked myself while writing this section in an effort to identify my strengths and so figure out how to tell others how to discover their strengths. In asking myself this, I realized that I might actually know my strengths.

272   Experts believe Benjamin Franklin and Thomas Edison had ADHD.

ADHD. We have plenty of experience doing things at the last minute.[273]

Developing Strengths

Strengths are useless unless they are developed and used to their full potential. When one identifies a strength, it is imperative to develop it. Take the time to grow your strengths. I am sure we have all heard this advice before,[274] but are we actually implementing this idea in our lives? It is easy to say, "Yeah, I know that," but it is another thing entirely to follow through. Let this paragraph serve as a reminder to act.

Champions

Let us say for the moment that you have identified a strength and are in the process of trying to develop it. There may come a moment where doubt creeps into your mind. You might start to think it is not really a strength and you are just wasting your time. That is when it is vital to surround yourself with those who believe in you. They will inspire you to keep trying. We all (whether we have ADHD or not) need a champion in our lives–someone who believes in us and will take the time to help us achieve our goals. People who encourage us to do what we love doing inspire us in our moments of weakness. These are the people with whom we ought to be making a connection.

---

273   Did I just brag about doing things at the last minute? That is probably not something about which to brag.

274   I know I have, and to be honest, I am a little disappointed in myself for writing all of that. It seems trite and like old news.

CONNECTIONS

"We must consider how to rouse one another to love and good works. We should not stay away from our assembly, as is the custom of some, but encourage one another, and this all the more as you see the day drawing near." – Hebrews 10:24-25

Importance of Connections in Managing in ADHD

In their book, *Delivered from Distraction*, Doctors Edward Hallowell and John Ratey describe the importance of a connected life in managing ADHD. "Creating a connected life is the key to happiness and health," they write.[275] There is no need to feel down if you have ADHD. You have good inside you, and you have strengths.[276] Those with whom you make a connection can help you develop your strengths and make the right decisions in life.

Finding Connections

There are many types of connections a person can make, and Hallowell and Ratey list many in their afore-mentioned book. One of the first connections a person makes in his/her life and one that the Church teaches is the building blocks of society[277] is the family. Another family-like connection a person makes is friendship. The symptoms of ADHD can make familial relationships and friendships difficult to maintain.[278] We ADHDers need to put in extra effort to make these relationships work, but the rewards of the extra effort are worth it.

Doctors Hallowell and Ratey also list other connections one can make throughout the community. They say it is crucial for a person to feel welcomed, respected, and fairly treated at their school and/or workplace. Moreover, they encourage people to get involved in activities, clubs, and organizations that interest them. These connections make a person feel needed, build self-esteem, and are often fun. Piggybacking off of this idea, I would add getting involved in your parish to Hallowell and Ratey's list of connections.

Two of the connections on Doctors Hallowell and Ratey's list are focused on God's creation. One is nature which, according to Hallowell and Ratey, allows a person an opportunity to feel relaxed, draw joy and inspiration, and have a place to play. My favorite item on his list of connections is pets. Hallowell and Ratey state that pets can be one of the greatest sources of warmth and happiness. I have also heard Doctor Hallowell state in interviews that, if it were up to him, every child with ADHD would be given a puppy when they were given their diagnosis.[279]

---

275   It should be noted that, although they wrote it in a book about ADHD, this advice is applicable to anyone regardless of whether or not they have ADHD.

276   See previous chapter.

277   "As the family goes, so goes the nation, and so goes the whole world in which we live." – Saint John Paul II

278   I discuss relationship struggles more in the chapters "What Is ADHD?" and "Everyday Life Struggles."

279   One of the key reasons he believes this is how taking care of a pet can teach a child responsibility.

Lastly, Doctors Hallowell and Ratey's list includes two connections that I think are crucial to creating a connected life that will help overcome the challenges presented by ADHD. The first is something he refers to as "the spiritual world." I am sure he calls it this, so it applies to people of all beliefs. But, because I am writing a book about ADHD from a Catholic perspective, I will call a spade a spade: The most important connection you can make is your relationship with God. Your prayer life must be a priority. The second key connection is the one you have with yourself. I discuss in many places throughout this book the myriad of self-esteem challenges a person with ADHD faces. It is important that you do not allow the negative self-talk to which ADHDers are prone to ruin the relationship you have with yourself. Accept your weaknesses, embrace your strengths, and deal with lingering issues from your past.[280] God loves you, so you should love you too.

A Criminological Interlude

A fun fact about the author of the book you are reading is that I have a master's degree in criminal justice. My focus while pursuing this degree was the analysis of criminal behavior. I bring up my criminology background because I believe some of the work criminologists have done in explaining criminal behavior supports Doctors Hallowell and Ratey's belief that strong, healthy connections are key to overcoming the challenges presented by ADHD.

One such criminologist is Edwin Sutherland. His differential association theory reflects his belief that crime is learned. Sutherland proposed that some people commit crimes because of the associations they make with others. Years later, another criminologist, Ronald Akers, built upon differential association and formulated his social learning theory. Akers added details on how the learning in differential associations takes place. He noted that those with whom criminals (or potential criminals) associate can help the would-be offender form favorable opinions of criminal behavior or opinions that justify criminal behavior. Also, Akers stated that another way the learning of criminal behavior occurs is through imitation. Potential offenders witness the criminal behavior of their associates and then imitate their behavior and become criminals themselves.[281] What we can take away from Sutherland's differential association theory and Akers' social learning theory is that the connections we make, whether good or bad, will influence our behavior.[282] If we associate with the right people and organizations, it will be easier to form better habits with regards to our behavior, especially ones where ADHD makes it tempting to make the wrong choice.

Another criminological theory worth exploring is Travis Hirschi's Social Bond Theory. Hirschi put forth the idea that external social bonds help explain why people do not commit crimes. He described four different types of bonds people make that prevent them from committing a crime. The first is "attachment," which Hirschi described as caring about what others think about you. The second bond is "commitment," those personal investments one

---

280   This might mean seeking out a therapist.

281   The assigned reading, while we were exploring these theories, included two articles about crimes that must be learned to be committed. One was how one needs to learn how to properly smoke marijuana for the drug to have an effect on the user. The other gave an inside look at the training prostitutes receive.

282   This is, of course, assuming that this theory reflects reality.

has made. These include jobs, schooling, family, clubs, sports teams,[283] etc. Hirschi's third bond is "involvement." The idea behind the third bond is that, if one is involved in activities or is otherwise kept busy, one will not have time to offend. The final bond Hirschi describes is "belief." Hirschi opined that the belief system one has or has been taught will affect their attitude towards crime. If one is brought up to abhor a certain crime, one will not commit that crime. On the other hand, if one comes to believe music should be in the public domain, one will have no reservations about pirating music. In applying the ideas of Hirschi's social bonds theory to ADHD and the idea of connections, we can see a similarity between his advice and Hallowell and Ratey's advice. It is the connections we make that help keep us on the straight and narrow, help us find a healthy place in life, and lead us to grow as individuals.

---

283   This refers to sports teams of which the individual in question is a member, not teams the individual watches on TV.

HOW TO HELP SOMEONE WITH ADHD

"Amen, I say to you, whatever you did for one of these least brothers of mine, you did for Me." – Matthew 25:40

If You Have ADHD, Do Not Skip This Chapter![284]

Guess what? Other people have ADHD too. If you would like help from others, then it is only fair for others with ADHD to expect the same from you.

For Those of You Who Picked Up This Book to Help Someone You Love Who Has ADHD...

First of all, thank you. Those of us with ADHD appreciate those who seek to learn more about the crazy gift of the cross of ADHD. The simple fact that a non-ADHDer desires to know more about our struggles is heart-warming.

I could write eloquently about how to handle a person with ADHD, but how-to guides should be simple. For the sake of simplicity and so that you can easily refer back to this list when you need a refresher, I have written most of this chapter in list format. There is a special non-list section at the end of the chapter for any members of the clergy who may be reading this book.

DOs

• Learn about ADHD.[285] Ignorance helps no one. You cannot help with a problem of which you have no understanding.[286] We cannot receive assistance from you if you have no idea what you are talking about. Quite frankly, ignorance infuriates us.

• Acknowledge our strengths and help us to develop them. If we neglect our strengths and focus on our weaknesses, our emotional state will slip, and our self-esteem will sink.

• Help us find, maintain, and/or stick with a routine and/or structure, specifically one that works for us individually. Everyone experiences ADHD differently, and different strategies work for different people.

• Be open to being an accountability partner, but do not demand that we have an accountability partner. These relationships only work when they are freely chosen.

• Be patient with us. We will mess up, and it helps if you are patient with us when we do so.

---

284   You can skip this chapter temporarily but do come back to it later.

285   +10 points to you for reading this book.

286   No one completely understands ADHD, though. Those of us with ADHD do not always have a good understanding of ADHD, but we know where we struggle (well, most of the time). Bottom line: The more you know, the better. But, we will not demand that you become an expert on the subject.

• Demand excellence. We are not doomed to mediocrity. Help us remember that.

DON'Ts

• Do not shame us.[287]

• If we have a system or structure in place, do not mess with it. First of all, we will get angry, but it will also make us unproductive again. We might not regain that level of stability again for a long time.[288]

• Do not tell us ADHD is not real. We know ADHD is real. You cannot convince us otherwise; we have science on our side. Your ignorant Reddit post cannot change our minds.[289]

• Do not ask us to pray to be cured of our ADHD. It cannot be prayed away.

• Yelling and screaming at us does not help.[290] In fact, a 2017 study found that cutting back on harsh treatment of children with ADHD[291] improved their biological functioning.

• Do not force us to change. If you want us to change, that is great. It shows you care about us.[292] However, if we do not want to change, there is a good chance we will not try hard to change.

• Do not be a parent to us. Unless, of course, you are our parent. In that case, yes, be our parent, but do not be a helicopter parent. We need to learn how to adult at some point in time.

The Role of the Clergy in Ministering to Those with ADHD

A proper ADHD treatment plan encompasses multiple disciplines. Medication, therapy, coaching, diet, and exercise are all recommended by experts for helping manage the symptoms of ADHD. One thing that may be mentioned as an aside or in wishy-washy terms (such as "spirituality") is Faith. I am not saying one can pray away ADHD, but having a faith life can provide some benefit for those with ADHD. First and foremost, it can provide some sense of meaning to having something as difficult to endure as ADHD. Without Faith, ADHD becomes an unwelcome burden. Seen through the eyes of Faith, ADHD can be an avenue to grow closer to God.[293] However, growing closer to God can be difficult when one has ADHD. This is where the role of the clergy becomes crucial.

Those with ADHD need help from the clergy to grow in intimacy with God. I am not proposing every parish should have a ministry specifically for those with ADHD.[294] However, there are things the clergy can do in the

---

287 I really hope everyone who reads this book thinks, *Well, of course!* when reading this one.

288 It could be weeks or even months!

289 If I could reach through the computer and smack you...

290 It does not help your blood pressure either.

291 This study was only conducted on children with the hyperactive/impulsive presentation of ADHD, but I suspect the results would be the same for the predominately inattentive and combined types

292 It could also mean you view us as scum and wish we would stop being a burden to you. However, Jesus says in the Gospels to not be judgmental, so I will assume the best about you until you have given me indisputable evidence to the contrary.

293 See the chapter entitled, "Why Me?"

294 Although, if your parish wants to start one, I will not stop you. Where do I sign up?

ordinary course of their ministry to help those with ADHD.

First, it would be beneficial for the clergy to take steps to learn about ADHD and other mental health issues.[295] The understanding of mental health issues among the general population is disappointing, but when misinformation is expressed from the pulpit, it is completely demoralizing. The Good Shepherd knows His sheep intimately. How can priests represent Christ if they do not possess an adequate understanding of a good number of His flock?

Also, hardly anyone teaches how to pray. Everyone expects you to know how to pray, but how are we to know if no one teaches us? I would love to hear priests talk more about how to pray and how to improve one's prayer life. This would be beneficial for everyone, but it would help those with ADHD even more, especially if the lessons are specifically intended for those with ADHD and/or how to deal with distractions in prayer.

Moreover, explain what silence means in prayer. It cannot simply mean not thinking, can it? My brain does not do that. Those of us with ADHD are incapable of stopping thinking. How are we to achieve the silence that is often promoted in homilies, books, and lectures if we cannot halt our thoughts? We are told to be silent, but no one ever explains how to become silent.

It would also help those with ADHD if priests and deacons refrained from reading their homilies off of a piece of paper. These homilies are inevitably monotone and hard to follow, regardless of how magnificent the content is.[296] I want to pay attention, but the delivery puts me to sleep. You are supposed to be evangelizing, not reading us a bedtime story.

Lastly, the confessional is a place where an ADHDer needs their priest the most. In the confessional, we share our weakest moments. A person with ADHD will confess a lack of focus in prayer and giving in to the temptation to despair. In these moments, priests need to express compassion. They need to remind us of our dignity. Shame is an ever-present dark cloud in the life of a person suffering from ADHD.[297] A priest can do a tremendous amount of good by offering words of encouragement in the confessional. However, he needs to be prepared for this. No canned messages will do. Only true empathy will suffice.

---

295   +10 points to any member of the clergy reading this book.

296   Also, when a priest reads his homily off of a piece of paper, he closes himself off to the inspiration of the Holy Spirit.

297   So much so that I wrote an entire chapter of this book on shame.

REASONS FOR HOPE

"For I know well the plans I have in mind for you…plans for your welfare and not for woe, so as to give you a future of hope." – Jeremiah 29:11

Temptation to Give Up

The frustration those of us with ADHD feel with regards to focusing during prayer, at Mass, and in our daily lives can get intense. Failure is ever-present, looming over our shoulder waiting to rear its ugly head again. Sometimes, it feels like too much, and we feel like giving up.

Fighting the temptation to give up is a fight we must take up daily. Every single day I have worked on this book, I have fought that temptation. It is important to keep fighting, to keep striving for excellence even though giving up seems easier.

God Is with You

Let not your ADHD brain be troubled. I will not state in this paragraph that you can pray away the ADHD. Yes, God could take away your ADHD if He wanted to do so, but He almost always does not. In those instances, He does not because He has something better in mind for us. When struggles arise, ask God to help guide you through your struggle. He wants to help us, and He wants to hear about our struggles. Sometimes, our best prayers are the ones where we simply tell God what is going on in our life.[298] Yes, He knows what is going on in your life and how you feel about it, but He wants to hear it from you directly.

You Have Strengths

Finding your strengths is key to overcoming ADHD's challenges. Everyone has strengths, and when we find them and tap into them, amazing things can happen. I know that sounds cheesy,[299] but it is true.

Too often, those of us with ADHD focus on our flaws, shortcomings, and failures. Sometimes, we hyperfocus on our failures. Other times, we have been conditioned to think negatively about ourselves. One estimate concludes that children with ADHD could receive more than 20,000 negative or corrective messages in school by the age of 10.[lvii] This conditioning causes us to forget about our strong points.

Successful People with ADHD

Despite the numerous challenges those of us with ADHD face, we are not doomed to a life marred by a

---

298   As Saint Thérèse would say, "For me, prayer is a surge of the heart."

299   Part of me died when I wrote it.

series of one failure after another. There have been many individuals who have gone on to do great things. These individuals include:

- MLB great Pete Rose
- Popstar Justin Timberlake
- *Extreme Makeover: Home Edition's* Ty Pennington
- Maroon 5 lead singer Adam Levine
- Actor Channing Tatum
- JetBlue founder David Neeleman
- Olympian Michael Phelps[300]
- Entrepreneur Sir Richard Branson
- *Dancing with the Stars'* Karina Smirnoff
- Olympian Simone Biles
- Political commentator James Carville
- Television and radio host Glenn Beck
- ADHD expert and author Dr. Edward M. Hallowell
- Actor Jim Carrey
- Actor, comedian, and television host Howie Mandel
- Singer Solange Knowles
- Film director Alejandro González Iñárritu
- Actor Jim Caviezel[301]

Perseverance

As we fight the temptation to give up every day, we must remember the reasons for hope I listed above. It is hard when we fail to focus on prayer every time we pray, but we must keep praying. The most important virtue someone with ADHD can possess is perseverance. When the Devil tries to remind you how much you have and will fail him because of your ADHD, persevere. I try to remember that perseverance can be a prayer in and of itself: "If the heart wanders or is distracted, bring it back to the point quite gently and replace it tenderly in its Master's presence. And even if you did nothing during the whole of your hour but bring your heart back and place it again in Our Lord's presence, though it went away every time you brought it back, your hour would be very well employed." – St. Francis de Sales

---

300   Phelps has been outspoken about ADHD, depression, and other mental health issues. He has also opened his home to Olympic athletes who are struggling with adjusting after years of training for the Olympics and being unable to cope with returning to normal life.

301   You know, the guy who played Jesus in Mel Gibson's *The Passion of the Christ*

ACKNOWLEDGEMENTS

Jay Perry
Shaun McAfee
"Mrs. Palmer"
Fr. Kevin O'Dell
John Michels
Naomi Swing Design & Photo
My family and friends

Thank you all for believing in me

ABOUT THE AUTHOR

Alex R. Hey, PCAC is an ADHD coach and owns his own coaching practice, Reset ADHD. Just before his junior year of high school, he chose to start taking his faith seriously, and he has not regretted that decision. Hey was diagnosed with ADHD at the age of 20. The diagnosis explained two decades of underachievement and feeling misunderstood. His ADHD diagnosis did not immediately make life easier, however. He continued to search and grow. Now, Hey chooses to help others through his coaching practice and speaking engagements. He lives in Sioux Falls, SD with his two dogs, Charlie and Ace. To learn more about Alex R. Hey or his coaching practice, visit ResetADHD.com. To read more of his writing, visit alexrhey.com

Connect with Alex online:

Twitter: @ResetADHD or @A_R_Hey
Facebook: http://facebook.com/resetadhd
Instagram: @resetadhd
LinkedIn: https://www.linkedin.com/company/resetadhd/
Blog: ResetADHD.com/blog

ENDNOTES

[i] Massachusetts General Hospital. (2008, October 8). ADHD Stimulant Treatment May Decrease Risk Of Substance Abuse In Adolescent Girls; Results Mirror Findings In Boys. ScienceDaily. Retrieved July 21, 2017 from www.sciencedaily.com/releases/2008/10/081006180519.htm

[ii] Seidman, Larry & Valera, Eve & Makris, Nikos. (2005). Structural Brain Imaging of Attention-Deficit/Hyperactivity Disorder. Biological psychiatry. 57. 1263-72. 10.1016/j.biopsych.2004.11.019.

[iii] Valera, Eve & V Faraone, Stephen & Murray, Kate & Seidman, Larry. (2007). Meta-Analysis of Structural Imaging Findings in Attention-Deficit/Hyperactivity Disorder. Biological psychiatry. 61. 1361-9. 10.1016/j.biopsych.2006.06.011.

[iv] Rubia, Katya & Smith, Anna & Brammer, Michael & Toone, Brian & Taylor, Eric. (2005). Abnormal Brain Activation During Inhibition and Error Detection in Medication-Naive Adolescents With ADHD. The American journal of psychiatry. 162. 1067-75. 10.1176/appi.ajp.162.6.1067.

[v] Fassbender, C., Zhang, H., Buzy, W. M., Cortes, C. R., Mizuiri, D., Beckett, L., & Schweitzer, J. B. (2009). A lack of default network suppression is linked to increased distractibility in ADHD. Brain Research, 1273, 114–128. http://doi.org/10.1016/j.brainres.2009.02.070

[vi] Flora, S.R., & Polenick, C.A. (2013) Effects of sugar consumption on human behavior and performance. The Psychological Record, 63, 513-524. doi:10.11133/j.tpr.2013.63.3.008

[vii] This estimate comes from New York University professor of psychiatry Len Adler, M.D.

[viii] Chamberlain, S., Ioannidis, K., Leppink, E., Niaz, F., Redden, S., & Grant, J. (2017). ADHD symptoms in non-treatment seeking young adults: Relationship with other forms of impulsivity. CNS Spectrums,22(1), 22-30. doi:10.1017/S1092852915000875

[ix] Genizi, J., Marom, D., Srugo, I., & Kerem, N. (2014). EHMTI-0013. The relations between attention deficit and hyperactivity disorder and different types of headaches in a non- clinical sample of adolescents. The Journal of Headache and Pain, 15(S1). doi:10.1186/1129-2377-15-s1-b10

[x] Jensen, C. M. (2016). ADHD in Danish children and adolescents: Incidence, validity, psychiatric comorbidity, and antisocial outcomes. Aalborg Universitetsforlag. Ph.d.-serien for Det Humanistiske Fakultet, Aalborg Universitet

[xi] Kessler, R. C., Adler, L., Barkley, R., Biederman, J., Conners, C. K., Demler, O., . . . Zaslavsky, A. M. (2006). The Prevalence and Correlates of Adult ADHD in the United States: Results from the National Comorbidity Survey Replication. American Journal of Psychiatry, 163(4), 716-723. doi:10.1176/ajp.2006.163.4.716

[xii] Kessler, R. C., Adler, L., Barkley, R., Biederman, J., Conners, C. K., Demler, O., . . . Zaslavsky, A. M. (2006).

The Prevalence and Correlates of Adult ADHD in the United States: Results from the National Comorbidity Survey Replication. American Journal of Psychiatry, 163(4), 716-723. doi:10.1176/ajp.2006.163.4.716

[xiii] Anxiety and Depression Association of America

[xiv] Anxiety and Depression Association of America

[xv] Kessler, R. C., Adler, L., Barkley, R., Biederman, J., Conners, C. K., Demler, O., . . . Zaslavsky, A. M. (2006). The Prevalence and Correlates of Adult ADHD in the United States: Results from the National Comorbidity Survey Replication. American Journal of Psychiatry, 163(4), 716-723. doi:10.1176/ajp.2006.163.4.716

[xvi] Masi, L., & Gignac, M. (2015). ADHD and Comorbid Disorders in Childhood Psychiatric Problems, Medical Problems, Learning Disorders and Developmental Coordination Disorder. Clinical Psychiatry, 1(1). doi:10.21767/2471-9854.100005

[xvii] Kessler, R. C., Adler, L., Barkley, R., Biederman, J., Conners, C. K., Demler, O., . . . Zaslavsky, A. M. (2006). The Prevalence and Correlates of Adult ADHD in the United States: Results from the National Comorbidity Survey Replication. American Journal of Psychiatry, 163(4), 716-723. doi:10.1176/ajp.2006.163.4.716

[xviii] Kessler, R. C., Adler, L., Barkley, R., Biederman, J., Conners, C. K., Demler, O., . . . Zaslavsky, A. M. (2006). The Prevalence and Correlates of Adult ADHD in the United States: Results from the National Comorbidity Survey Replication. American Journal of Psychiatry, 163(4), 716-723. doi:10.1176/ajp.2006.163.4.716

[xix] Mayo Clinic

[xx] National Institute of Mental Health

[xxi] Kotte, A., Joshi, G., Fried, R., Uchida, M., Spencer, A., Woodworth, K. Y., . . . Biederman, J. (2013). Autistic Traits in Children with and Without ADHD. Pediatrics, 132(3). doi:10.1542/peds.2012-3947

[xxii] Davis, N. O., & Kollins, S. H. (2012). Treatment for Co-Occurring Attention Deficit/Hyperactivity Disorder and Autism Spectrum Disorder. Neurotherapeutics, 9(3), 518-530. doi:10.1007/s13311-012-0126-9

[xxiii] Jensen, C. M., & Steinhausen, H. (2014). Comorbid mental disorders in children and adolescents with attention-deficit/hyperactivity disorder in a large nationwide study. ADHD Attention Deficit and Hyperactivity Disorders, 7(1), 27-38. doi:10.1007/s12402-014-0142-1

[xxiv] Sibley, M. H., et al. (2011). The Delinquency Outcomes of Boys with ADHD with and without Comorbidity. Journal of Abnormal Child Psychology, 39(1), 21–32. http://doi.org/10.1007/s10802-010-9443-9

[xxv] Steinhausen HC, Novik TS. ADORE Study Group. Co-existing psychiatric problems in ADHD in the ADORE cohort. Eur Child Adolesc Psychiatry 2006; 15: I/25-I/29.

[xxvi] Srirangam Shreeram, Jian-Ping He, Amanda Kalaydjian, Shannon Brothers, Kathleen Ries Merikangas, Prevalence of Enuresis and Its Association With Attention-Deficit/Hyperactivity Disorder Among U.S. Children: Results From a Nationally Representative Study, In Journal of the American Academy of Child & Adolescent Psychiatry, Volume 48, Issue 1, 2009, Pages 35-41, ISSN 0890-8567, https://doi.org/10.1097/CHI.0b013e318190045c.

[xxvii] Baeyens, D., Roeyers, H., Demeyere, I., Verté, S., Hoebeke, P. and Walle, J. V. (2005), Attention-deficit/ hyperactivity disorder (ADHD) as a risk factor for persistent nocturnal enuresis in children: A two-year follow-up study. Acta Pædiatrica, 94: 1619–1625. doi:10.1080/08035250510041240

[xxviii] Robson, W. L., Jackson, H. P., Blackhurst, D., & Leung, A. K. (1997). Enuresis in children with attention-deficit hyperactivity disorder. Southern medical journal, 90(5), 503-505.

[xxix] Kessler, R. C., Adler, L., Barkley, R., Biederman, J., Conners, C. K., Demler, O., . . . Zaslavsky, A. M. (2006). The Prevalence and Correlates of Adult ADHD in the United States: Results from the National Comorbidity Survey Replication. American Journal of Psychiatry, 163(4), 716-723. doi:10.1176/ajp.2006.163.4.716

[xxx] Fasmer, O. B., Halmøy, A., Oedegaard, K. J., & Haavik, J. (2011). Adult attention deficit hyperactivity disorder is associated with migraine headaches. Eur Arch Psychiatry Clin Neurosci, 261, 595-602. doi:10.1007/s00406-011-0203-9

[xxxi] Mayo Clinic

[xxxii] Kessler, R. C., Adler, L., Barkley, R., Biederman, J., Conners, C. K., Demler, O., . . . Zaslavsky, A. M. (2006). The Prevalence and Correlates of Adult ADHD in the United States: Results from the National Comorbidity Survey Replication. American Journal of Psychiatry, 163(4), 716-723. doi:10.1176/ajp.2006.163.4.716

[xxxiii] Kessler, R. C., Adler, L., Barkley, R., Biederman, J., Conners, C. K., Demler, O., . . . Zaslavsky, A. M. (2006). The Prevalence and Correlates of Adult ADHD in the United States: Results from the National Comorbidity Survey Replication. American Journal of Psychiatry, 163(4), 716-723. doi:10.1176/ajp.2006.163.4.716

[xxxiv] Mayo Clinic

[xxxv] Mayo Clinic

[xxxvi] Mayo Clinic

[xxxvii] Kessler, R. C., Adler, L., Barkley, R., Biederman, J., Conners, C. K., Demler, O., . . . Zaslavsky, A. M. (2006). The Prevalence and Correlates of Adult ADHD in the United States: Results from the National Comorbidity Survey Replication. American Journal of Psychiatry, 163(4), 716-723. doi:10.1176/ajp.2006.163.4.716

[xxxviii] Masi, L., & Gignac, M. (2015). ADHD and Comorbid Disorders in Childhood Psychiatric Problems, Medical Problems, Learning Disorders and Developmental Coordination Disorder. Clinical Psychiatry, 1(1). doi:10.21767/2471-9854.100005

[xxxix] Kessler, R. C., Adler, L., Barkley, R., Biederman, J., Conners, C. K., Demler, O., . . . Zaslavsky, A. M. (2006). The Prevalence and Correlates of Adult ADHD in the United States: Results from the National Comorbidity Survey Replication. American Journal of Psychiatry, 163(4), 716-723. doi:10.1176/ajp.2006.163.4.716

[xl] Steinhausen HC, Novik TS. ADORE Study Group. Co-existing psychiatric problems in ADHD in the ADORE cohort. Eur Child Adolesc Psychiatry 2006; 15: I/25-I/29.

[xli] Masi, L., & Gignac, M. (2015). ADHD and Comorbid Disorders in Childhood Psychiatric Problems, Medical Problems, Learning Disorders and Developmental Coordination Disorder. Clinical Psychiatry, 1(1).

doi:10.21767/2471-9854.100005

[xlii] Sibley, M. H., et al. (2011). The Delinquency Outcomes of Boys with ADHD with and without Comorbidity. Journal of Abnormal Child Psychology, 39(1), 21–32. http://doi.org/10.1007/s10802-010-9443-9

[xliii] Mangeot, S., Miller, L., McIntosh, D., McGrath-Clarke, J., Simon, J., Hagerman, R., & Goldson, E. (2001). Sensory modulation dysfunction in children with attention-deficit–hyperactivity disorder. Developmental Medicine & Child Neurology, 43(6), 399-406. doi:10.1017/S0012162201000743

Mathison, Jason, "Sensory Processing in Children with ADHD: A Classroom Study and Rational Item Analysis" (2012). PCOM Psychology Dissertations. Paper 212.

Ghanizadeh, Ahmad. (2011). Sensory Processing Problems in Children with ADHD, a Systematic Review. Psychiatry investigation. 8. 89-94. 10.4306/pi.2011.8.2.89.

[xliv] Masi, L., & Gignac, M. (2015). ADHD and Comorbid Disorders in Childhood Psychiatric Problems, Medical Problems, Learning Disorders and Developmental Coordination Disorder. Clinical Psychiatry, 1(1). doi:10.21767/2471-9854.100005

[xlv] Masi, L., & Gignac, M. (2015). ADHD and Comorbid Disorders in Childhood Psychiatric Problems, Medical Problems, Learning Disorders and Developmental Coordination Disorder. Clinical Psychiatry, 1(1). doi:10.21767/2471-9854.100005

[xlvi] Kessler, R. C., Adler, L., Barkley, R., Biederman, J., Conners, C. K., Demler, O., . . . Zaslavsky, A. M. (2006). The Prevalence and Correlates of Adult ADHD in the United States: Results from the National Comorbidity Survey Replication. American Journal of Psychiatry, 163(4), 716-723. doi:10.1176/ajp.2006.163.4.716

[xlvii] Masi, L., & Gignac, M. (2015). ADHD and Comorbid Disorders in Childhood Psychiatric Problems, Medical Problems, Learning Disorders and Developmental Coordination Disorder. Clinical Psychiatry, 1(1). doi:10.21767/2471-9854.100005

[xlviii] Retz, W., Stieglitz, R.-D., Corbisiero, S., Retz-Junginger, P., & Rosier, M. (2012). Emotional dysregulation in adult ADHD: What is the empirical evidence? Expert Review of Neurotherapeutics, 12(10), 1241-1251. http://dx.doi.org/10.1586/ern.12.109

[xlix] Bush, G., Frazier, J. A., Rauch, S. L., Seidman, L. J., Whalen, P. J., Jenike, M. A., . . . Biederman, J. (1999). Anterior cingulate cortex dysfunction in attention-deficit/hyperactivity disorder revealed by fMRI and the counting stroop. Biological Psychiatry, 45(12), 1542-1552. doi:10.1016/s0006-3223(99)00083-9

[l] Allman, J. M., Hakeem, A., Erwin, J. M., Nimchinsky, E. and Hof, P. (2001), The Anterior Cingulate Cortex. Annals of the New York Academy of Sciences, 935: 107–117. doi:10.1111/j.1749-6632.2001.tb03476.x

[li] Dodson, W. (2018, April 03). How ADHD Ignites Rejection Sensitive Dysphoria. Retrieved May 23, 2018, from https://www.additudemag.com/rejection-sensitive-dysphoria-how-to-treat-it-alongside-adhd/

[lii] Luke 18:10-14

[liii] Wright, J. P., Tibbetts, S. G., & Daigle, L. E. (2014). Criminals in the Making: Criminality Across the Life

Course (2nd ed.). Thousand Oaks, CA: SAGE Publications, Inc.

[liv] Langevin, R., & Curnoe, S. (2011). Psychopathy, ADHD, and Brain Dysfunction as Predictors of Lifetime Recidivism among Sex Offenders. International Journal of Offender Therapy and Comparative Criminology, 55(1), 5–26.

[lv] John 16:33

[lvi] Bell, Ziv & Shader, Tiffany & Webster-Stratton, Carolyn & Reid, Jamila & Beauchaine, Theodore. (2017). Improvements in negative parenting mediate changes in children's autonomic responding following a preschool intervention for ADHD. Clinical Psychological Science. 10.1177/2167702617727559.

[lvii] Jellinek, M. S. (2010, May 1). Don't Let ADHD Crush Children's Self-Esteem. Retrieved September 12, 2017, from http://www.mdedge.com/clinicalpsychiatrynews/article/23971/pediatrics/dont-let-adhd-crush-childrens-self-esteem